OVER THE LAST THIRTY years, thoughtful Christian leaders have realized the importance of the Holy Spirit to help us move beyond institutional division and inertia. Genuine renewal of the church and of the individual requires an integrated understanding and practice of the Holy Spirit in our personal lives and in decision making as congregations and denominations. We have long needed both a workable theology of the Holy Spirit and encouragement in the daily practice of receiving this wonderful gift. Trevor Hudson does just that. He helps us to learn about the Holy Spirit and to experience the Holy Spirit as the living presence of God. No one can read this book without feeling a nudge.

—Jerry P. Haas
Coauthor with Trevor Hudson, *The Cycle of Grace*

SURPRISINGLY, FEW HAVE WRITTEN in a way that brings together Christian spiritual formation and the work of the Holy Spirit in the life of a believer. Trevor Hudson's *Holy Spirit Here and Now* does just this. If you are looking for a book that "normalizes" the work of the Spirit in your daily life; if you have ever been traumatized by seeking for certain special effects of the Charismatic movement; or if you simply long for intimate interaction with God, this is a wonderful book for you.

—Gary W. Moon, M.Div., Ph.D.
Executive Director, Martin Institute and Dallas Willard Center
Westmont College
Author, *Apprenticeship with Jesus*

IN MY EXPERIENCE, books on the Holy Spirit tend either to be too simple to deal adequately with the wonder and mystery of this person of the Trinity or so complex that they are of little value to anyone other than the academic Christian theologian. This book is a wonderful exception! In its pages Trevor Hudson has drawn on a rich tapestry of deep personal experience of the person and work of the Holy Spirit in his own life and ministry. This experience is strengthened and supported by a wealth of robust theological research. What made these insights particularly helpful for me was that they brought the experience and theology of the Holy Spirit together in a wonderfully deep, practical spirituality. I would highly recommend this volume for any serious seeker after God. Whether you long for a fresh encounter with God in the Holy Spirit, or you have been afraid or simply uninformed about the person and work of the Holy Spirit, this book has some wonderful treasures for you.

—Dr. Dion A. Forster
Lecturer, Ekklessia—Stellenbosch University, Faculty of Theology

IN LIFE YOU GET authors whose books you want to read—every single one of them. For me, Trevor is one of those people and this book does not disappoint. Theologically it is well grounded; it stays true to the Tradition. But at the same time it surprised me—it invited me to a new kind of engagement with the Holy Spirit.

—Johan Geyser
Cultural architect of Mosaiek Church

In this inspiring book Trevor takes us by the hand and leads us gently. Not only closer to God but also encouraging the reader to embrace, without fear, the awesome presence of the Holy Spirit within them. A must-read for every believer longing for more of God's love and power in his or her life.

—Christine Ferreira
Editor, *Lééf met hart & siel*

HOLY SPIRIT

HERE AND NOW

Trevor Hudson

UPPER
ROOM BOOKS®

The Upper Room website: http://www.upperroombooks.org

Unless otherwise indicated, scripture quotations are from the Holy Bible, New International Version®, NIV®. Copyright © 1973, 1978, 1984, 2011 by Biblica, Inc.™ Used by permission of Zondervan. All rights reserved worldwide. www.zondervan.com

Scripture quotations noted NRSV are from the New Revised Standard Version Bible, copyright © 1989 National Council of the Churches of Christ in the United States of America. Used by permission. All rights reserved.

At the time of publication all websites referenced in this book were valid. However, due to the fluid nature of the Internet some addresses may have changed or the content may no longer be relevant.

Cover design: Ellen Parker Bibb/ellenparkerbibb.com

Library of Congress Cataloging-in-Publication Data
Hudson, Trevor, 1951–
Holy Spirit here and now / Trevor Hudson.
pages cm
ISBN 978-0-8358-1220-7 (print)—ISBN 978-0-8358-1221-4 (mobi)—ISBN 978-0-8358-1222-1 (epub)
1. Holy Spirit. I. Title.
BT121.3.H83 2013
231'.3—dc23

2012041075

As always, for

Debbie, Joni, and Mark

*and all those who have mentored me
in the life of the Spirit*

CONTENTS

ACKNOWLEDGMENTS

Thank you for reading this book. It means a great deal to me that you would take the time. Writing *Holy Spirit Here and Now* was a long, challenging, and stretching journey. It would not have been completed without the prayers, insight, and loving encouragement of many people in my life. So let me acknowledge with much gratitude and appreciation the following:

To Jeannie Crawford-Lee, Rita Collett, and Joanna Bradley (editorial staff); to Debbie Gregory and Nanci Lamar (production staff); to Janice Neely, Lauren Hirsch, and Anne Trudel (marketing staff)—thank you for your gifts of colleagueship, collaboration, and competence along the way to publication and beyond. I have greatly valued my partnership with Upper Room Books, which has now seen the publishing of seven of my books over the past nine years. Your collective support, wisdom, and care have been invaluable.

To Glen Lester, Jacque Borman, Marina Fick, and Gavin Sklar-Chic who prayed for this book during its writing—thank you for inquiring about the book's progress and for your constant reminders that you were holding this writing project in your prayers.

To Marilyn Dorrington who helped me proofread early copies of the manuscript—thank you for your interest in the book and for your hidden ministry in the library of the Northfield Methodist Church.

To each of those companions along the way, both within and outside the church who have shared their faith-stories with me—thank you for encouraging me to become more open to the Spirit of God in my own faith journey.

To Richard Foster, John Ortberg, Gary Moon, Jerry Haas, Dion Forster, Johan Geyer, and Christine Ferreira who read the manuscript and offered comments—thank you for the time, effort, and thought that you gave to this task.

To David Smolira, SJ, who has accompanied me with his listening presence on my own spiritual journey over recent years—thank you for helping me recognize and respond to the Holy Spirit's work in my life during this transitional phase in my life and ministry.

To Scot McKnight for writing such a gracious and generous foreword—thank you for your writings that constantly inspire, challenge, and guide me into a deeper discipleship with Jesus Christ.

To Joni Hudson and Mark Hudson, wonderful companions with whom to share the delights and struggles of life—thank you for your willingness to continue hanging out with your Dad and for helping me to become lighter, freer, and more joyful in spirit.

To Debbie Hudson, my soul mate, whose presence means home for me—thank you for your faithful love, never-ending grace, and steady faith through which the Holy Spirit touches my life daily. I am deeply blessed.

—Trevor Hudson

FOREWORD

From the moment the church got its start at Pentecost, all the way to the end of the Book of Acts, the Holy Spirit is at work. In the New Testament the Holy Spirit isn't simply one of the three persons of the Trinity. Like the Father and the Son, the Spirit is alive and at work, and the church folks like Peter, Stephen, and Paul knew the Spirit and saw the Spirit.

Pick up one of the letters of the apostle Paul, First Corinthians, for example, and watch what happens: The Spirit works among the believers in the churches, convicting them, healing them, and promoting their growth. So much so that each one of those Christians received a gift, a skill if you like, a unique offering of each for the good of all in the church. The Spirit was equipping.

This active Spirit we see in the New Testament is taken up anew by Trevor Hudson, one of South Africa's strong Christian leaders. He expresses the Spirit's work among us through active verbs like "bringing us alive," "transforming us," "guiding us," "leading us into the desert," and "engaging us with suffering."

The only way to talk about the Spirit in a healthy, biblical way is to talk about what the Spirit is *doing* rather than what we believe about the Spirit or even how the Spirit relates to the Father and to the Son—each important in its own sphere of thinking. But first and foremost the Spirit is at work, pursuing activities, turning us around abruptly and slowly, and then changing you and me into the sort of people who look more and more like Christ. The Spirit creates space for us in the worldwide body of Christ so that we might all work together. The Spirit connects us to one another at the deepest levels and then draws us out of ourselves to love others as Jesus did.

This Spirit resides in us at the smallest and most intimate levels and at the same time works in us, the body of Christ in the world, as the agent of new creation. I choose to read Trevor Hudson's wise, discerning, and challenging book because I know he's been doing the hard work of being humbled by life, by God's work and word, and by God's Spirit. He has appropriated the spiritual disciplines that Dallas Willard and Richard Foster teach so well. This book presents ideas that emerge from the soul of a man who wants God's Spirit to work in him. This man has stories to tell of the Spirit's action in this world—the Spirit improvising today as the Spirit acted at the beginning, the same Spirit at work today.

I pray this book will lead you to be more open to God's Spirit at work in your life and in our world.

—Scot McKnight
Professor of New Testament
Northern Baptist Theological Seminary

Why Another Book on the Holy Spirit?

Why write another book about the Holy Spirit?" a close friend asked me when I told him I was writing this book. It is a good question. Many books about the Holy Spirit are readily available. I have benefited from reading several of them. Yet for some time now I have wanted to write about how the Holy Spirit works in our lives. Several reasons come to mind.

First, I know that many people feel like second-class Christians when it comes to an awareness of the Holy Spirit. They hear others speak confidently about their experiences of the Spirit, either at church or while viewing religious TV programs. They feel left out of such happenings. These people often end up thinking that experiences of the Holy Spirit come to religious professionals or those inclined to charisms or the really weird—but not to them. You may be one of these. If you are, I hope this book will help you recognize the Holy Spirit's work within you at this moment.

Second, I meet people who have been through off-putting, scary, and painful experiences related to the Holy Spirit. I think of my mother who seldom went to church. On one occasion when she attended, well-meaning people took her into a side room and prayed for her "to receive the Spirit." She felt tremendously pressed to speak in tongues. This event traumatized her. Only years later, in response to the gentle, accepting, and thoughtful ministry of one of my colleagues, did she willingly return to a church.

Perhaps you have had a similar occurrence so that now, whenever someone raises the topic of the Holy Spirit, you become defensive. I can understand this. However, you may be robbing yourself of good and important experiences that God desires for you. So I hope you will consider some of the lessons about the Holy Spirit that I have been learning over the past forty years. You do not need to be afraid. More than anything else, the Holy Spirit wants you to know that you are infinitely loved by a good and loving God whose human face we have seen in Jesus Christ.

A third reason for writing is because I meet many spiritual seekers who are looking for "something more" in their relationship with God. They are tired of a superficial, shallow, and secondhand faith. They long for intimate interaction with the living God. They yearn to know the fire of God's presence burning in their hearts. They know that unless God becomes a living reality for them, they may as well throw in the towel when it comes to their relationship with God. After all, when we do not experience God's life within us, our Christianity often deteriorates into a lifeless system of dreary rules and empty rituals.

If the above describes you at the moment, know that you are not alone. Ever since I began following Jesus at the age of sixteen, I have sought a deeper, closer, and more power-filled experience of God. This search has taken me down many different pathways. Some have turned out to be dead ends. Others have been useful for a time. One or two have proven themselves enduringly helpful. I hope that in sharing some of these experiences with you, I will guide you down some practical and life-giving avenues in your search for a real sense of the living God in your life.

Fourth, I want to bridge the deep chasm that often exists between our experience of God's Spirit and our everyday lives. Many of us tend to confine our encounters with the Holy Spirit to the religious zone of our lives: worship moments, Bible study groups, and church conferences. As a result, we don't recognize the activity of the ever-present Spirit in our personal struggles or in our messy and muddled relationships or in our nine-to-five jobs with all their stresses and strains or in the overwhelming social challenges that we face. We think that we have to leave our material day-to-day lives behind and enter the so-called "spiritual" world of church activities to experience the Holy Spirit. The consequences of this dual approach are tragic. We develop a split spirituality and usually end up living double lives.

One thing I want to convey about the Holy Spirit is this: The Holy Spirit is continuously at work in *all* of our lives, from our very beginnings, in every encounter, in our daily work, in our communities, indeed throughout the whole universe. I hope this conviction will become clearer as you read this book. When we can recognize the Holy Spirit at work in and around us and respond to this divine activity, we begin to heal the tragic gap between our relationship with God and what happens in our everyday lives. Rather than trying to make religion our life, our life becomes our religion. The effects are life-transforming.

Lastly, I want to hold out a vision of our relationship with God as an invitation to go on a lifetime journey with the Holy Spirit. Too often, we interpret Paul's command to be filled with the Holy Spirit as having a singular experience that we live off forever. I want to suggest a different approach. This challenging instruction by the apostle invites the Holy Spirit's total renovation of who we are. It challenges us to allow every part of our lives—our hearts, our minds, our emotions, our bodies, our souls, our relationships, our work—to become arenas where the Holy Spirit can work. Only then are we truly filled with God's Spirit. Are you willing to embark on this Spirit-propelled adventure of restoration, renewal, and transformation?

I trust that at least one of these reasons connects with where you are at this moment. If so, I hope you will read on. In this exploration into who the Holy Spirit is and what it is that the Holy Spirit does, I will turn frequently to what the biblical writers said about these matters. I will share some stories of my own struggles and joys in my attempts to be more responsive to the Holy Spirit, as well as reflect on some of the encounters that friends and colleagues have had with the Holy Spirit. At the end of each chapter, I will describe a simple practice that will help you interact more intentionally with the Holy Spirit. I follow this practice with some thoughts that might lead to good conversation and group sharing if you are reading this book with others.

May the Holy Spirit be with you as you read! Here is one of my favorite prayers that you might like to pray as you begin.[1]

Spirit of God,
Lord and Giver of Life,
moving between us and around,
like wind or water or fire;
breathe into us your freshness that we may awake;
cleanse our vision that we may see you more clearly;
kindle our senses that we may feel you more sharply;
and give us the courage to live
as you would have us live,
through Jesus Christ our Lord.
Amen.

ONE

The Gift God Gives

Returning from an overseas ministry trip, I stopped overnight in Zurich. While there I decided to go into the city center to find a gift for my wife, Debbie. When I entered a shop to buy her a skirt, I faced problems. The shop assistant could not speak English, and I could not speak German. I did my best to describe Debbie's figure with my hands. This did not help. Then I showed her a photograph of Debbie. This did not help either. As a last resort, I tried to explain with homemade sign language that I would try the skirt on myself.

Let me quickly say that I am not usually this brave when it comes to buying gifts. By nature I am a rather shy person. However, being similar in height to Debbie I knew that if the skirt fitted me, it would also probably fit her. So I went into the ladies' changing room, closed the curtains of the small cubicle, and put the skirt on over my jeans. When I came out to show the surprised assistant and to ask whether it fit, she had gathered all the other assistants together to see this strange cross-dresser from South Africa!

We sometimes go to amazing lengths to select a special gift for a loved one. We spend large amounts of money. We invest much time looking for the right present. We keep secrets in order to surprise the other person. Some of us willingly make complete fools of ourselves to ensure that the gift is suitable (like my trying on a skirt in a women's dressing room). Sometimes I wonder who receives the more joy from gifts—the one who gives or the one who receives.

Consider the meaning of giving and receiving gifts. On one hand, gifts express our love. When we love people, we want to give our loved ones something special. We want to show them how much they mean to us. In a sense, we give ourselves through the gifts we give. On the other hand, when we receive a thoughtful gift, we realize how much we mean to another person. The more personal the gift we receive, the more it touches our heart. Sometimes we are so moved by what we have been given that we find it difficult to express our appreciation and gratitude.

This was my experience on my sixtieth birthday. I opened my family's carefully wrapped birthday gift to find a photograph album of my life with photos of my childhood family, my growing-up years, my close friends and mentors, my significant moments over the years, and so much more. My family's love overwhelmed me. As I paged through the album, I became aware of the huge effort, the thoughtfulness, and the many hours they had spent in putting it together. I felt enfolded in my family's love. How does one say thank-you in moments like this?

THE HOLY SPIRIT AS GOD'S GIFT

I begin in this way because the Bible often describes the Holy Spirit as the gift of God. Recall the encounter between Jesus and the Samaritan woman at the well. "If you knew the gift of God . . . " (John 4:10), Jesus said to her. He went on to speak to her of living water. Elsewhere he draws an analogy between water and the Holy

Spirit[1] that has led many to believe that Jesus' statement refers to the Holy Spirit. Furthermore, in the first sermon recorded in the book of Acts, Peter says to those who repent, "You will receive the gift of the Holy Spirit" (Acts 2:38). Other biblical allusions to the Holy Spirit use the term "the heavenly gift" (Heb. 6:4) and more simply the "gift" (Acts 11:17) given to the apostles at Pentecost.

But what does it mean to describe the Holy Spirit as the gift of God? Exploring this question gets us thinking more deeply about who the Holy Spirit is. We also begin to wonder about that great mystery we call the Trinity—one good God exists as a community of Father, Son, and Holy Spirit. But I do not want us only to increase our knowledge about the Spirit. I hope by engaging this question thoughtfully, we will open ourselves to the gift that God wants to give us all. So let me begin with three convictions about the Holy Spirit as the gift of God that will undergird this book.

MORE THAN AN "IT"

During the '70s and '80s some readers may recall an explosion of interest in the Holy Spirit around the world. The so-called charismatic movement brought renewal to the lives of millions of Christ-followers. Many people, including myself, found themselves experiencing God in a new, fresh, and living way. Strikingly, a number of church leaders in South Africa who stood at the forefront of the struggle against apartheid at that time also participated in this wave of the Spirit. Involvement in the struggle for justice taking place on the streets required an empowerment that only the Spirit could give.

This interest in God's Spirit also manifested unhelpful aspects. Its focus on experiencing the Spirit led many into a search for mere spiritual thrills. We may find ourselves easily titillated by various phenomena when it comes to openness to the Spirit. Congregational division surfaced around these phenomena. One negative aspect was the casual way in which people sometimes referred to the Spirit. I still remember being asked, "Have you got *it?*" I never felt sure of how to answer. While I knew the person was referring to the Holy Spirit, sometimes I would jokingly say, "Of course, I have got *it.* Why do you think Debbie married me?"

Speaking of the Holy Spirit as an "it" suggests that the Spirit is some kind of invisible force or impersonal power or abstract influence. However, if this were really so, we would be unable to relate personally to the Spirit. Nor could the Holy Spirit guide, comfort, or lead people, which the Bible describes as activity of the Spirit. But even more sadly, regarding the Holy Spirit as an "it" encourages people to do and say some terrible things; often manipulating others to bring about certain desired effects.

GOD'S PERSONAL PRESENCE

The Bible invites us to see the Holy Spirit as a person and in a personal way. To offer one example, Jesus underscored the Spirit's personhood when he assigned to the Holy Spirit the title "advocate" (John 14:16). In Greek this title implies that the Holy Spirit will be for us in the present what Jesus has been for his disciples during his life on earth. Thus, the Holy Spirit will be our friend, leader, and guide just like Jesus had been for those who knew him in Galilee. But this relationship can be true only if the Holy Spirit is God's personal presence in the here and now.

I hope this delineation is clear. When God gives us the Holy Spirit, God gives us nothing less than God's own self—an important emphasis. The Holy Spirit is God here today, present with you and me, right now. Some other metaphors and symbols used in the Bible to describe the Holy Spirit—words like *water, fire, breath, wind*—can sometimes suggest that the Holy Spirit is only "something divine." But the Holy Spirit moves far beyond an impersonal "something" to be a "Someone." When we cry out from our depths, "Come,

Spirit, come," we are crying out for the Lord to come and personally fill our lives.

Our understanding of the Holy Spirit in personal terms leads us to recognize how the Holy Spirit enables our experience of God's active and immediate presence. Later exploration will note Bible teachings about how the Holy Spirit's activity brings us alive to God's presence, draws us into a deeper shared life, changes us inwardly, guides us in our decision making, helps us to pray, empowers us for witness, and so on. Consider the list of activities carefully. These actions are not taken by an impersonal "it." They are *personal* actions of the living God at work within our lives, right where we are.

Many of us desire an experience of God as a living personal reality. Theories about God do not satisfy the deep longings of our hearts. We have grown tired of a faith that does little more than moralize, intellectualize, or advise. We want a two-way relationship with God that will make a difference in our daily lives. We want to know Christ as a vibrant indwelling presence working within and through us. To put it bluntly: We want to encounter God.

For this reason God bestows the gift of the Holy Spirit, God's personal presence in the here and now. The question is whether you and I will open our lives to receive the gift of God.

GOD LOVING US NOW

The finest gift we can offer someone dear to us is the gift of our love. When we fall in love, our actual love for that person is our primary gift to him or her. As the relationship grows and matures over time, our love continues to be our most special gift to the other person. Nothing else can take its place. The reason for this is obvious. When we give someone our love, we give *ourselves* to him or her, which makes our gift so meaningful to those close to us.

This understanding is equally true in our relationship with God. God's best gift to us is God's love for us. The writer of First

John arrives at this conclusion after spending a lifetime in relation-ship with God. (Read 1 John 4:7-16.) Notice that he does not say God *has* love but rather that God *is* love. Our God is extravagantly, sacrificially, passionately loving. Indeed, this is the bottom line of the Christian faith when we reflect on our relationship with the God who has come to us in Jesus Christ. God actively loves us.

Elsewhere I have written of how the meaning of this truth for our lives can be illustrated from nature. We can compare God's love to the sun. It is the sun's nature to give warmth and light. The sun always shines, always radiates its warmth and light. The sun cannot act against its essential nature. Nor can we can stop it from shining. We can allow its light to fill our senses and make us warm; alter-nately, we can separate ourselves from its rays by putting up an umbrella or going indoors. But whatever we may do, we know that the sun does not change its essential nature.

In the same way, the God revealed to us in Jesus always loves. Like the shining sun, God's love never ceases. In every moment of our lives, God sends out the warm rays of divine love. This is where the Holy Spirit comes in. If the sun represents God in Jesus Christ, we could say that the sun's rays represent the Holy Spirit. So to be touched by the Holy Spirit is to be touched by God's love. Likewise, to be filled with the Holy Spirit is to be filled with God's love. Paul makes this connection when he writes, "God's love has been poured out into our hearts through the Holy Spirit"(Rom. 5:5).

This insight that links the gift of the Holy Spirit with God's continually radiating love receives repeated confirmation in the expe-riences of ordinary people. Here is an excerpt from an e-mail sent by a young adult after someone had prayed for him following a worship service. He had come forward to the altar rail after my speaking about the Holy Spirit's assurance of God's love.

> *Throughout most of my life I have felt very lonely. When you asked God to fill my life with the Holy Spirit, that feeling went away. I felt myself immersed in the ocean of God's love. Since*

Sunday the sense of God's love for me has not left me. I know
like never before that my life is wrapped in God's love.

Special experiences like this can lead to spiritual breakthroughs, but by themselves they seldom transform our hearts or our character. What happens as people experience the Spirit in large Christian gatherings is often temporary. The everyday routines of their relationships and work lives cannot sustain the highly charged emotional and spiritual atmosphere of these events. Thankfully, though, the Spirit brings us God's love in many everyday ways.

EVERYDAY HOLY SPIRIT MOMENTS

Think of how we experience God's love each day in the ordinary moments of our lives. God's love comes to us in every gift we receive. In the sun that warms us, the water we drink, the food we eat, the energy we use, the stranger who greets us; indeed, in our very existence. We can truly receive the gift of the Holy Spirit when we inhale the air we breathe or feel the light of the sun on our faces or wash our bodies with water or delight in the life we live. These are "Holy Spirit moments" of God loving us in the midst of our everyday lives.

But most often the Holy Spirit ushers God's love into our lives through those who love us. One recent experience stands out for me. I was on a ministry trip overseas, speaking at a conference. Each day I would be picked up from the hotel where I was staying. After giving my talk, I would then be dropped off at the hotel. It was a very lonely time. One morning, while praying in the shower, I asked God to give me a reminder of God's love. About thirty minutes later, I received a text message from my wife, Debbie. Because of the difference in time zones, I knew it was about two in the morning in South Africa. Fearing that something bad had happened back home, I opened the message rather anxiously. It turned out to be a very special gift. It read as follows:

Just want to let you know that I love you. Wish you were here
so that I could give you a hug. Hope your day goes well.

You may say, "An amazing coincidence." I don't think so! For me it was a Holy Spirit moment. Our human love for one another gives expression to the Holy Spirit's presence. Where love is, God is present, for God is love and love is of God. Whenever we express love to someone, God's Spirit works through us to convey God's love to that person. When we receive love from someone, God's Spirit works through that person to bring God's love to us. We need to become more aware of the Holy Spirit's bearing God's love into our lives.

God bestows the gift of the Holy Spirit who is God loving us in the here and now. The question is whether you and I will open our hearts to this gift of God.

GOD'S GRACE ACTIVE IN US

When we speak about the gift of the Holy Spirit, we move into the realm of God's grace. The Bible clearly links the Holy Spirit and grace. The two actually come together in one place where the writer to the Hebrews speaks of "the Spirit of grace" (10:29). Some scholars have pointed out that in many places in the New Testament we can exchange the words. Where *Holy Spirit* is written we can read *grace*, and where we find the word *grace* we can read *Holy Spirit* without altering the text's meaning.[2] You may choose to look up some of these passages on your own.

This link suggests that whenever we experience the Holy Spirit, we experience grace, and the other way round. This insight turned my understanding of grace upside down. For a long time I saw grace merely as a lifeless theological idea. But when I began to make these connections between the Holy Spirit and grace, they helped me to see matters differently. Grace is a real power, in the same way that the Holy Spirit is a real power. We could state it like this: God's grace is the Holy Spirit acting in our lives helping us to accomplish those things that we cannot accomplish in our own strength.

This support comes in several ways. To begin with, the Spirit of grace works in our lives from the moment we come into existence. For many years I mistakenly thought that the Holy Spirit only started working in my life after my conversion. It was a special moment when I realized that the Holy Spirit had been reaching out to me with God's love long before I made my first commitment to Christ. Now I have come to see that even when I made a decision to follow Jesus, it was the Holy Spirit who had stirred up my longing for him. God's grace had been seeking me all the time, and I had been unaware of it.

Furthermore, we experience the Spirit of grace when we consciously trust Christ for the first time. As you may already know, some powerful things happen in this critical moment. We realize that Christ is Lord. We become conscious of our desperate need for God and reconnect with God as our heavenly Parent. We are made aware of the realities of God's kingdom and receive assurance that we are God's beloved children. We are adopted into God's family. We did not deserve or achieve or earn any of these things. They are all gifts of God's grace given by the Holy Spirit who continuously works in our lives.[3]

After conversion we need and experience the Spirit of grace even more deeply! As we seek to be faithful to God in the new life to which we've committed ourselves, the Holy Spirit gives us power beyond our own resources. For example, once we have given ourselves to Christ, we develop a new desire to live open, truthful, and transparent lives. But this desire will not be lived out in our own strength. When we try to follow Christ on our own, we fail again and again. We know this from our own experience. As we yield our lives consciously to the Holy Spirit, God's grace gradually shapes us into the persons we long to be.

So let me ask: Do you feel that you are experiencing the Spirit of grace at the moment? If not, here is the way forward. Invite the Holy Spirit into whatever task you may want to do with God. Hopefully, this will include all that you do through the day. Ask often for the Holy Spirit's help as you try to live the abundant life that the Bible describes. You can simply pray, "Lord, help me with your Spirit in this task" or "Lord, let your Spirit change my heart" or "Lord, may your Spirit guide me in this matter." These simple prayers will open more widely the doors of your life to experience the Holy Spirit on a daily basis.

Now we can also see how persons who follow Christ depend on the Holy Spirit's grace so much. My friend and mentor Dallas Willard supplies an analogy to explain this truth in a practical way: An aircraft racing down the runway before takeoff uses up much more fuel than the one standing still in the airport's hangar. Similarly, when we remain content with our experience of God as it is, we park our faith in the hangar. But when we seek Christ wholeheartedly and want more of his reign in our lives, we begin to move down the runway. As we do so, the Spirit of grace empowers us to take off. We begin to accomplish things that we cannot accomplish in our own strength.

This is why God bestows the gift of the Holy Spirit—God's grace active in our lives in the here and now. Again the question becomes whether you and I will open our lives to this gift of God.

NOTICING

All this talk about the Holy Spirit does not mean that we sit back and do nothing. Little occurs when we do nothing in our lives with God. Experiencing more of the Holy Spirit requires involvement. God's love and grace is opposed to earning but is not opposed to effort! At the end of each chapter, I will describe a spiritual practice that will help us open our lives to God's love and grace in the here and now. Spiritual practices make it possible for us to live more deeply in the Spirit on a moment-to-moment basis.

Before I introduce you to the first spiritual practice, let me remind you of my three foundational convictions about the gift of God. The Holy Spirit is God's personal presence. The Holy Spirit is God loving us. The Holy Spirit is God's grace active in our lives. Put these three convictions together, and we can celebrate one bit of good news about God's Spirit: *Through the Holy Spirit, God is lovingly present and always active in our lives.*

Let us meditate on this good news. The Holy Spirit is at work in our lives in every encounter, in our daily work, in our communities, and indeed throughout our whole universe. We experience the Holy Spirit all the time. The Spirit of God always reaches out to us with God's love and grace in moments of beauty, love, rest, joy, and newness. The Holy Spirit touches us—even in our pain, disappointment, grief, struggle, and loneliness. We simply recognize and respond to this ever-present activity of the Holy Spirit. At this point, the first spiritual practice of *noticing* comes in.

One way to begin this practice entails setting aside a block of time to pursue the following exercise. Let me describe it as fully as I can. Go back over your life and *notice* how the Holy Spirit has been with you over the years. Make a list of significant moments when you have felt loved, cherished, and valued. Then try to *notice* the gifts of love and grace that you have received in your life. Write these on a piece of paper. Finally, ask God to help you notice how the Spirit has encouraged growth in your relationship to the divine. Be as specific as possible. Throughout the exercise express your feelings and thoughts to the Father, the Son, and the Spirit, asking them to deepen your awareness of their presence in your life.

When I first worked through this exercise, I came to a massive realization: The Spirit had been active in my life long before my conscious choice to become a Christ-follower. As I spent time looking back, I began to recognize that the Holy Spirit had been present throughout my life, continuously bringing God's love to me, touching my life with grace, and stirring up desire for God. I believe this is true for us all. As the psalmist prays, "Where can I go from your Spirit? Where can I flee from your presence?" (Ps. 139:7).

Once we have completed this exercise, we can further grow our capacity to notice God's Spirit by looking back over the day each evening. We play the day back in our imagination and try to notice where the Spirit has touched our lives. Maybe we enjoyed a moment of human love, a moment when it felt good to be alive, a moment when it seemed as if God was using us to help someone else. Maybe we experienced the touch of the Spirit over a cup of coffee, some help given by a colleague, an encouraging text message, a piece of work well done, or some other moment we appreciated. These moments are gifts of God's love and grace, signs of the Holy Spirit at work in our lives. Noticing them allows us to experience the Holy Spirit who was lovingly present and active in them.

By using this practice of daily review on a regular basis, we will fine-tune our ability to receive and acknowledge the Spirit as events occur through the day. We will begin to receive the Spirit in every breath we take, every bite of food we eat, every hug we receive, every person we meet. Even in difficult and painful moments we will find ourselves able to receive God's love and grace. Nothing can stop God from loving us! Is this not part of what Paul meant when he shared his conviction with his readers in Rome that nothing in all creation could separate us from the love of God in Christ Jesus our Lord?

Right now, as you read these words, you can receive the Spirit. Right now, as you feel the chair you are sitting in, as you think about what you are reading, as you look around where you are, you can receive God's love and grace. Right now! As noticing the activity of God's Spirit becomes a natural part of your everyday life, you will open yourself to experience the Holy Spirit in the here and now, which is just how God wants it to be. For after all, the Holy Spirit is the gift of God given to each one of us.

SMALL-GROUP CONVERSATION STARTERS

Icebreaker: What was the most special gift you received as a child?

1. Write the words *Holy Spirit* on a sheet of newsprint. Brainstorm your immediate responses to these words. Record all these under the name *Holy Spirit.*

2. What are your earliest memories of God's love and grace in your life?

3. What has been your most recent experience of God's love and grace?

4. What would it mean for you if you recognized the Holy Spirit as active in these experiences of God's love and grace?

5. What practice would help you notice more often the Holy Spirit's work in your everyday life?

TWO

. . . Brings Us Alive to God's Presence

This is how the Holy Spirit brought me alive to God's presence. My family of origin did not have prayers or say grace at meals or go to church. The only time I can remember attending Sunday worship during my growing-up years was when I went with my dad to a Remembrance Day service. It was an evening Anglican service, and we sat near the back in the darkened sanctuary. When my dad went forward for Communion, I stayed behind in the pews, feeling quite scared and alone. I felt relieved when he returned!

In tenth grade I changed schools. In my new classroom, I found myself seated next to Philip, with whom I became good friends. We played rugby together, slept over at each other's homes, and had long conversations about life, love, and everything else. After a short while, it became clear to me that Philip understood and lived his life in a radically different way. God seemed real and present in his life. His faith was more than talk. He wanted to please God in all he did. This God-reality gave his life an unusual depth of purpose and direction. One day as we walked home together from school, I asked, "Philip, what makes your life different?"

Very simply, Philip introduced me to his relationship with Jesus Christ. He shared how Jesus had died for our sin, told me about his resurrection, and explained how his Spirit comes to live in our lives today. He went on to say that if I wanted to experience God's presence, I needed to turn toward Jesus and give my life to him. Basic street-level theology opened my heart and mind to God's good-news story. I knew I had a decision to make. For the first time in my life I began to consider that Jesus wanted me not only to believe in his existence but also to trust and follow him.

Late one night, I walked home down Havelock Street in my hometown of Port Elizabeth. I recall looking up to the night sky and saying something like, "Lord Jesus, thank you for everything that you did for me. I give myself to you. I want to follow you for the rest of my life. Please come into my life, and make me the person you want me to be." The following evening I attended a Youth for Christ evangelical rally. The speaker invited those who wanted to follow Christ to come forward. Because I felt unsure about my request the night before, I walked down the aisle and knelt at the front rail. My journey with Jesus into life with God had begun.

Following that decision, Jesus seemed to step out of the mists of history and into my life as my living friend and guide. When I spoke with him in prayer, I experienced a new awareness of God in my life. I began reading the Bible with fresh eyes. I started with the letter to James and sought to put into practice what I read. I sensed a new desire within me to avoid evil, to do what was good, and to please God. Philip took me to a nearby Methodist Church where I formed friendships with other followers of Jesus. I started worshiping with others for the first time, even though I don't sing too well. I began seeing people as infinitely precious and sacred. In a nutshell, I discovered that turning toward Christ had brought God's presence alive in my life. The Holy Spirit was at work!

CONVERSION

Later I learned that what had happened to me is called conversion. *Conversion* is an old-fashioned word, shunned by many, valued by others. People use it to describe the radical change of heart that God's Spirit works in us when we put our confidence in Jesus Christ. Our lives become aimed in a totally new direction. We have a new "Christ focus." We develop a new awareness of the Abba-Father heart of God. While we could also use other biblical phrases like "being born from above" (John 3:7, NRSV), a crossing over "from death to life" (John 5:24) to describe this experience of coming alive to God's presence, I will stick with the concept of *conversion*. If you find this word off-putting, I hope that you will give me some grace and stay with me.

In this chapter I want to explore ways in which the Holy Spirit works in this experience we call conversion. It is important that we do this. When we put all the emphasis on what *we* do, critical as our part may be, we can subtly end up thinking that we convert ourselves. However, the New Testament insists that conversion is first and foremost an action of God's Spirit in our lives. Think of Paul's words as one example of this insistence: "No one can say, 'Jesus is Lord,' except by the Holy Spirit" (1 Cor. 12:3). So how does the Spirit of God bring us alive to divine presence?

DRAWS US TOWARD CHRIST UNIQUELY

First of all, the Holy Spirit brings us alive to God by drawing us toward Christ in a unique way. In the previous chapter we emphasized the Holy Spirit's presence and activity in our lives since our very beginnings. From our birth, God has been wooing us, calling us, seeking to awaken us from our spiritual sleep. In all the experiences and encounters of our lives, the Holy Spirit has been at work trying to create in us an awareness of God's desire for relationship. Often we glimpse this divine activity only when we look back at the events of our lives before we made the decision to give ourselves to Christ.

When I look back over my life, I can discern many signs of the Holy Spirit's work prior to my conversion. I recognize the Spirit of God going before me in the economic struggles surrounding my decision to change schools; through the coincidence of Philip sitting next to me; in Philip's caring concern for me, in his witness to Jesus, and also in my own restless longings to find purpose and meaning for my life. While I lacked awareness then of God's love and grace reaching out to me, now I recognize that through these actions the Holy Spirit was drawing me toward Jesus Christ.

God's Spirit probably worked in a different way in your life before your conversion. This should not be surprising. Not only are we created uniquely in relationship to God, but the circumstances of our lives differ. We come from different backgrounds, have different family histories, represent different cultures, and speak different mother tongues. It seems only right therefore that our conversion stories would be different. The Holy Spirit works in the same manner in our lives but always approaches that work uniquely.

There is another important difference. For some people, this initial turning to Jesus comes suddenly and dramatically, as it did for me. People who experience this kind of turning moment can usually give precise details of how, when, and where they were converted. Their conversion story involves life before Christ and life after Christ. Often a radical break with destructive habits of previous life accompanies a strong sense of starting over again. When we hear stories in the church of people coming to faith, more often than not it is these conversion stories that we hear.

For others, their turning toward Christ comes more gradually, taking place in what seems to be small stages over a length of time—even years. This is often the experience of those who have grown up in Christian homes, who have been exposed to Jesus' story for as long as they can remember, and who have never wandered too far from the family of God. They cannot tell you exactly when they began to follow Christ, but they know they are following him at this moment. We do not often hear these conversion stories in our churches. As a result, these folks may feel that their conversion experience is somehow inferior to those who are converted more dramatically.

In whatever happened before you turned to Christ, whether your turning moment was sudden or gradual, you can be sure of the Holy Spirit's involvement. Reflecting on your unique conversion story will help you become more aware of this fact. Here are some questions that may help you in this reflection:

- What life circumstances led up to your conversion?
- What God-incidences happened?
- Who did God bring across your path that prompted you to begin thinking about your relationship with God?
- How did you first become aware of God's love and grace?
- How did you hear about the call to follow Christ?

Your responses to these questions will help you see more clearly how God's Spirit worked in your life to draw you to Christ.

I realize that as you think about these matters, you may wonder whether you are converted or not. Let me just say this: If at this moment your heart is turned toward Christ and you are consciously seeking to trust and follow him, then you can be sure conversion has taken place. If you are not consciously trusting and following Christ, you may discover that the Holy Spirit is trying to get your attention and encouraging you to respond more consciously to the call of Jesus Christ in your life.

WORKS THROUGH GOD'S GOOD-NEWS STORY

Second, the Holy Spirit works through God's good-news story to bring us alive to God's presence, another essential ingredient of the conversion process. We turn toward Christ and give ourselves to him when the gospel of God's love and grace touches our hearts and minds. At this point, God's Spirit enters. The Holy Spirit makes the story of God's salvation-drama relevant to each of our lives. Whether this happens suddenly in a dateable and definable way or gradually over a long period of time, the result is the same. We find ourselves falling in love with God and entrusting our lives and wills to Jesus Christ as deeply as we are able.

When we refer to God's good-news story, it helps us keep the big picture in view. This drama begins with God creating a beautiful universe, including our planet, including human life, including you and me. The Genesis accounts of Creation issue strong overtones of God's passionate, generous, and cherishing love. The Spirit hovers over the shapeless state of the universe like a mother bird protecting and nurturing the new life beneath her. Eventually, on the sixth day, human beings come into the picture. They are given the special assignment of looking after the earth, loving each other, and living in a loving relationship of interactive responsibility with God.

However, matters go very wrong. Our first parents refuse to let God be God in their lives. They prefer to be their own gods, to control their own lives, and to go their own way. The results of this rebellion lie all around and within them. Although physically alive, they die spiritually through disconnection from the true homeland of their souls. They allow self-interest and self-will to sabotage their relationships and find themselves imprisoned in a cell of willful self-centeredness, unable to break free. The results of their selfishness continue through their descendants. Above all, they fail to become the people God wants them to be. It does not take much imagination to recognize their story as our own.

Thankfully, God's good-news story does not end at this point. Beginning with Abraham, God sets up a rescue operation to restore creation to its original harmony. God calls a special people through whom God will bring this about. God promises to be with them every step of the way. This partnership between God and the nation of Israel is the story of the Old Testament—a messy story of triumph and failure, faithfulness and betrayal, glory and tragedy. Ultimately, God's chosen people fail to exercise their vocation as God's light to the nations. But in the darkness, a bright hope emerges that God will enter our world in a special way and complete Israel's calling to put creation back together again.

God does this in Jesus Christ. It is as if God draws near to us in Jesus Christ and says, "I am *Abba*, your heavenly parent. I love you beyond your wildest imaginings and yearn to share an intimate, conversational friendship with you. Your presence is desired at my family table more than you will ever know. Through the power of my Spirit in the earthly life of Jesus of Nazareth, I have shown you what it means to truly live with me. In his death, resurrection, and ascension, I have overcome all the powers of evil, sin, and death and have declared him to be Lord and Messiah of the universe. The new world of my reign is now available to everyone, and you can participate in it by learning to trust and follow Jesus.[1]

Whenever someone speaks meaningfully about God's good-news story, the Holy Spirit draws us into the divine drama of restoration and redemption. It always helps when the persons who share something of the story with us actually live in the story themselves. This is what happened in my relationship with Philip. Through his caring friendship, I experienced the story of God's love long before he spoke to me about it. When he did speak about Christ's love for me, it made sense because I had already seen the reality of it in him. His life had become for me a "fifth Gospel" in the story of God's love and grace, helping me believe that what was written in the four Gospels of the New Testament could be trusted.

As I have listened to other people's conversion stories, I have learned that the Holy Spirit can use any part of God's good-news story to get us started along the road of conversion. The Holy Spirit may work through a sudden awareness of God's love in creation, a Bible story in which we see ourselves clearly, a parable about God's amazing grace, a truth spoken by Jesus that pierces our heart, the incredible fact of Jesus dying on the cross out of love for us, the breathtaking news that Jesus lives beyond crucifixion, or the "fifth Gospel" of a friend's changed life.

What part of God's good-news story did the Holy Spirit use to convert you? Just today someone was telling me how his journey of faith began. He told me about going to church one Sunday evening still hungover from an all-night party. The preacher that night used the well-known text of the risen Christ standing outside the door of our lives, knocking. As my friend listened he realized that God was calling him to come home. That night he invited Christ into his life. This miracle happens whenever the Holy Spirit makes the story of God's love personally relevant to our lives and we willingly respond by placing our confidence in Jesus Christ.

GIVES OUR HEARTS A NEW RESPONSE OF LOVE

Third, the Holy Spirit brings us alive to God's presence by giving our hearts a new response of love. Let me explain what I mean. The essence of being alive comes in response. I was reminded of this the other day. I went to see our family physician for a checkup. At one stage of the process she asked me to sit on the side of the examining table. She then took a little hammer and tapped me just below my kneecap. There was an instant response. The lower part of my leg produced a healthy kick upward. She looked at me and said, "You are alive!" Indeed, being alive implies response.

When we experience conversion, the Holy Spirit produces in our hearts a new response of love. Our hearts awaken to God's incredible love. In return, we fall head over heels in love with God. We find ourselves looking for ways to receive God's love into our lives more deeply. We want to share God's love with those around us. As the song says, "Love changes everything." These changes take place when we open ourselves to God's good-news story. We begin to change from within and experience what we could call a Holy Spirit heart transplant.

In the Bible the metaphor of the heart represents that deep hidden core from which our deepest responses and choices come, the wellspring of our lives, the meeting place between God and us. In God's good-news story, the Old Testament prophet Ezekiel looked forward to the day when the people of God would receive new hearts to love God, to love others, and to act in new ways. He made it clear that all this would happen through the operation of the Spirit. Through the ancient prophet, God said these words: "I will give them an undivided heart and put a new spirit in them; I will remove from them their heart of stone and give them a heart of flesh" (Ezek. 11:19).

Think about this metaphor for a moment. Hearts of stone are hard, cold, and unresponsive. They want nothing to do with God. They lack a sense of awe, wonder, and reverence and struggle to love unselfishly. They are often unaware of the needs of those around them. Sometimes, according to scripture, stony hearts can be found in those who claim to belong to God's people. Stony hearts may foster judgmentalism, superiority, self-righteousness. Jesus seemed to have his most difficult times with religious people who were hard and heartless. Perhaps he still does.

In contrast, hearts of flesh are warm and responsive, reacting to God's longing for an intimate relationship in wholehearted sur-render to the Divine Love. We return God's love, and our hearts cry out in worship and loving adoration, "*Abba*, Father" (Rom. 8:15). The passionate desire of converted hearts is to be aligned with God's desires, whatever those may be. They move beyond selfishness and self-centeredness into a transformed way of being with others. Sensitive to human cries, they are attentive, they take notice, they respond. When hearts of flesh form within us, we come alive to the presence of God and others in a new way.

This complete change of heart is an inside job that the Holy Spirit initiates. The process begins when we open ourselves to the personal and passionate love that God has for each one of us, and we start to return that love. As we have already seen, the Holy Spirit brings us an awareness of God's good-news story in many ways. More often than not, we become aware of the depths of God's love expressed on the Cross. The Holy Spirit brings home to our hearts the knowledge that we are loved, accepted, and forgiven. To use the words of John Wesley, we find that our hearts have been "strangely warmed." In response we fall passionately in love with God and Jesus Christ and want to live with and for them alone.

Embodying this new love and new heart in the ups and downs of daily life is a lifelong learning journey involving the Holy Spirit and us. As we shall see in the next chapter, we never arrive! Even though my conversion took place over forty years ago, I continue to find pieces of hard stone in my heart. There are still moments when I forget God and want to be at the center, to be in control, to handle matters in my own way. Often I get discouraged by these struggles to love unselfishly those close to me. But I have learned to return to Christ who never gives up on me. I keep myself open to his spirit, confess my failure to love, and continue to trust that God will complete the heart transplant that was begun in me long ago. And, through all of this, my love for God has deepened and grown more than I can describe.

Our nations cry out for people with new hearts. A good friend and colleague went with a delegation of church leaders from different denominations to express concerns with some leaders of the ANC-led (Africa National Congress) government about the frightening levels of crime and corruption in South Africa. He later shared with me in a personal conversation. He said that after listening to the church spokespersons, one of the political leaders responded with these words:

> When we came to power, we promised you a new constitution. We delivered on our promise. You promised us people with new hearts. Where are they?

Reflect for a moment on the condition of your heart. How real is your love for God? Is your heart one of stone or of flesh? Allow Jesus, the great searcher of hearts, to search you within. What matters most to God is not our religiosity but whether our hearts are alive and responding in love to God and to others, beginning with those closest to us. I find myself asking the Holy Spirit to keep changing my heart. After all, conversion is a journey that continues throughout our lives.

But again, I must state that conversion will not occur without our cooperation. We are not robots that God simply rewires without consent. While the Holy Spirit is the key agent in our conversion, we also need to respond. Sometimes people refuse to do this. They prefer lives disconnected from God's presence. I have a hunch you would not be reading this book if this were the case. So let me share a practice that we need to build into our lives if we are going to experience conversion in ever-deepening ways.

REPENTANCE

By now we have seen that God's Spirit does not bring us spiritually alive without our cooperation. New life seldom, if ever, comes to the passive. We play a special part in our heart's conversion. We learn this from Jesus himself. When he preached his first message about God's gospel, he told his hearers that they needed to repent. (See Matt. 4:17; Mark 1:15.) From then on, repentance was one of his most consistent themes. Throughout the Gospels, he emphasized repentance as the doorway into our journey with God *and* the pathway along which we continue to walk.

Repentance involves turning toward God. It brings reconnection with God and redirection of our lives. Usually it encompasses a broken heart for the way we have lived without God, remorse for the ways we have wandered away from God, and now a new desire to love God and to live for God. "Repentance" is the translation of the Greek word *metanoia*. It means rethinking our lives, the complete turnaround of our mind and outlook, and a new willingness to place God at the center of our lives. We once refused to let God be God; when we repent, we now want God to be God in our hearts, our relationships, and our work. The outcome of true repentance is always joy—the deep joy of knowing that we are reconciled and restored to God's family.

A primary aspect of repentance is its ongoing nature. Many layers of consciousness reside within us, and on our journey of conversion we constantly discover new pockets of self-centeredness, willfulness, and selfishness. Such discoveries, explains one of my favorite writers, signal growth and progress along the spiritual way—not failure.[2] Christ's call to repent invites us to recognize these pockets of sinfulness and then to abandon ourselves anew to God. As our surrender to God deepens, the Holy Spirit gets to work on our stubborn hearts, bringing them more and more alive to God's presence in the process.

You can practice a moment of repentance right now. Ask the Holy Spirit to remind you of how God has reached out to our world. Imagine Jesus looking at you with love from the cross. Bask for a few moments in God's love streaming toward you from the Crucified One. Remind yourself that God is head over heels in love with you and that nothing can deter that love. I have come to realize that we can be more honest with ourselves and with God if we first accept that we are loved with a divine love that will never let us go.

Now think back over the last day or so and invite the Holy Spirit to bring into your awareness moments when you have not been responsive to God and to those around you. Perhaps it occurred when you acted out of deliberate self-interest or when you failed to understand another person's point of view or when you spoke unkindly and without thought to someone close to you. Once this moment is clearly fixed in your mind, turn again toward Christ, confess your failure, and yield yourself to the transforming work of the Spirit. Receive again the gift of God's love and forgiveness.

Try to build this practice of repentance and self-examination into your daily walk with God. If we want to come alive to God in the power of the Holy Spirit, we must continue to face those bits of stone in our hearts. This confrontation does not mean we are trying to fix ourselves up. Conversion is far more radical than any self-improvement job. It does mean, however, that we allow the Holy Spirit to change our hearts on a daily basis. Repentance—facing up to ourselves as honestly as we can, turning toward Christ with open hands, and accepting his personal love—creates the space for God's Spirit to do this deep inner work.

I realize that some who read this chapter believe that they have not yet begun the journey of conversion. You can begin right now, right where you are. You do not need to tidy up your life first and get everything in order. We never trust in our own goodness but in the power of God's love to change us. It is simply a matter of turning toward Christ with an open and transparent heart and surrendering yourself to him. That old familiar hymn puts it so well: "Just as I am, without one plea. . . . O Lamb of God, I come." As you practice your first act of repentance, I pray that you will experience the Holy Spirit bringing you alive to God's presence in your life in a wonderful way.

SMALL-GROUP CONVERSATION STARTERS

Icebreaker: What were your earliest feelings around the name *God?*

1. How do you understand conversion?
2. What life circumstances led to your coming alive to God for the first time?
3. What part of God's good-news story first impacted your life?
4. Name one way your heart has been influenced by the Holy Spirit.
5. How do you need the Holy Spirit to touch your heart at this moment?

THREE

THE GIFT GOD GIVES

. . . Draws Us into a Deeper Shared Life

For over thirty-five years I have followed the call to be a pastor. Alongside the vocational commitment to proclaim and teach God's good-news story, I have one other sacred ministry task. Almost daily—around kitchen tables, beside hospital beds, in counseling interviews, around the altar rail—I have gained access on a one-to-one basis into the struggles and yearnings of everyday people. This immense privilege merits my profound gratitude. Reflecting on these confidential pastoral conversations clarifies what I consider to be a deep yearning of the human heart: an earnest longing to belong.

Not to belong feels terrible. This explains why being lonely and disconnected from others brings such pain. We are not meant to live that way. The Bible affirms our making in the image of the one God who lives eternally in the community life of the Father, Son, and Holy Spirit. We are divinely designed by a relational God for intimate connection with God and with one another. We are made by love, in love, for love. Hidden in your heart and mine resides a capacity to give and to receive in our relationships with God and people. That capacity makes you and me human. When belonging happens, we move toward health, wholeness, and joy. When it does not occur, our souls suffocate, wither, and despair. You may know from your own experience what I am speaking about here.

The purpose of God's coming among us involves the experience of a new sense of belonging. Notice how the writer of First John makes this clear: "We proclaim to you what we have seen and heard, so that you also may have fellowship with us. And our fellowship is with the Father and with his Son, Jesus Christ" (1:3).

I must confess that when I first read this verse I was a little disappointed. Did Jesus come, live, die, rise, ascend, and pour out his Spirit just so that we could have *fellowship*? *Fellowship* has become such a weak and vague word in the English language. It calls to mind coffee in church halls, shaking hands at church doors, and making conversation with people we don't want to be with. Was this really the reason God sent Jesus Christ into our world?

THE TWIN DIMENSIONS OF KOINONIA

Then I learned that the Greek word used here for fellowship is *koinonia.* This word is rich, robust, and rigorous. The root meaning of *koinonia* is "to have in common, to share a common life." Fellowship, therefore, may involve many aspects: intimate sharing between persons, partnering together in a shared task, being with others from different backgrounds, a generous sharing of our economic resources. We catch a glimpse of these different shades of meaning when we read how the early Christ-followers related to one another after the Holy Spirit had come upon them at Pentecost. In Acts 2 we read that they spent time studying together, enjoyed meals together, prayed together, and shared their belongings with one another, according to what each one needed. The key word associated with the coming of the Spirit in all these verses is undoubtedly *together*. (See Acts 1:14; 2:1, 6, 44, 46.)

Notice also the author's emphasis that *koinonia*, created by the proclamation of God's good-news story, has two interconnected dimensions: a *horizontal* sharing of life among Christ-followers as well as a *vertical* sharing of life with the Father and the Son. Our fellowship is with God *and* with each other. When we open our lives to Jesus, he enters with his arms around his brothers and sisters. We find ourselves in a new community through which God wants to restore and bless those around us. We cannot say to Jesus, "I want to follow you, but I do not want anything to do with your sisters and brothers." That option is not open to us. What God has joined together, we dare not put asunder. The horizontal and vertical belong together as they always do in the symbol of the cross.

Looking back to the time when the Holy Spirit brought me alive to God's presence, I can see now how the Holy Spirit also joined me to others. Within a few days of giving my life to Christ, I found myself sharing life in a local congregation with other Christ-followers. I can still remember some of the names of those whom Jesus brought into my life: Eddie, Rose, Henry, Val, Charlie, Clem, David, Eric, Connie. Creating bonds of belonging among people who follow Jesus is one of the deepest ways in which the Holy Spirit works in our disconnected and isolated world. Hence, when Paul pronounces his blessing on the Corinthian church, he writes the following words: "May the grace of the Lord Jesus Christ, and the love of God, and the fellowship of the Holy Spirit be with you all" (2 Cor. 13:14).

I titled this chapter: *Draws us into a deeper shared life* because in this way the Holy Spirit fulfills the central purpose of God's good-news story. Every moment of our lives, in our every encounter, the Holy Spirit is seeking to connect us more securely with God and one another. I now want to suggest some ways in which the Holy Spirit does this. When we recognize the movements of the Holy Spirit in our lives, we can more ably respond to them. We can also be sure that as we follow these Spirit-prompted lead-ings, we will find ourselves connecting more deeply with those around us. Certainly this has been my experience as I have sought to keep my life open to God's Spirit. I hope that this will be your experience too.

WALKING IN THE LIGHT

The Holy Spirit draws us into a shared life by empowering us to walk in the light. We cannot walk in the light by our strength only. How often, especially within the setting of the church, do we tend to give the impression that we are more honest, more caring, more virtuous than we really are? In theory we may be willing to see the value of being open, honest, and transparent; but we seldom find it easy to put this theory into practice. Somehow it is easier to *pretend* to look good than to be good, to pretend to love than to love, to appear to be holy than to be holy. Rather than living in the power of the Spirit we become imposters of the Spirit.[1] A quick test: When did you last honestly share a weakness, sin, or struggle with a sibling in the faith?

God's good-news story will become our story only when we learn to walk in the light. Go back for a moment to those words from First John. Immediately after the writer stresses that fellow-ship is the purpose of God's good-news story, he notes the abso-lute necessity of walking in the light.

> *This is the message we have heard from him and declare to you: God is light; in him there is no darkness at all. If we claim to have fellowship with him and yet walk in the darkness, we lie and do not live out the truth. But if we walk in the light, as he is in the light, we have fellowship with one another, and the blood of Jesus, his Son, purifies us from all sin (1:5-7).*

These words are strong, sobering, and straightforward. They confirm the strong connections among walking in the light, having fellowship with one another, and receiving the cleansing that comes from Jesus Christ. When we pretend to be what we are not, we do not participate in a genuine shared life. As a consequence we do not fully experience God's love and grace, to which the blood of the Lamb points. However, when we live open, transparent, and honest lives, we walk in the light and have fellowship with God and one another. We also intensify the purifying power of Jesus Christ. But this experience comes only when the Holy Spirit empowers us to get honest, to take off our masks, and to begin to walk in the light of God.

Often I think those outside the church are more open to this empowering work of the Holy Spirit than those inside. The other evening I popped in to an Alcoholics Anonymous (AA) meeting that is held every Thursday evening in the church's fellowship hall. Some of my friends attend, and I wanted to see how they were doing. When I arrived, most of the recovering alcoholics were smoking outside the hall. Eventually we all went inside, and the meeting began. For the next two hours I listened as men and women shared their stories of betrayal, deceit, and pain. Some also related how they had come to the end of human resources, only to discover God meeting them at the end of their rope. The stories left me with a vivid realization of how the Holy Spirit changes us when we become more open and honest.

When I left the meeting, I stepped into the parking lot and looked around at our church's buildings. It is a church for which I have come to care deeply. Then I thought of the many church meetings that I have attended on the property. They differ greatly from the AA meeting. For a start, most meetings don't begin with all the members having a quick smoke beforehand! But I also thought about the often superficial sharing of struggles and sin that takes place with one another. As I stood next to my car, I asked God,

"Lord, where would your redemptive power be most at work on this campus—in the AA meeting or in those meetings that I attend?" Let me be honest with you, I didn't get an audible answer, but I sensed that the Holy Spirit whispered, "Usually in the AA meeting, because that's where men and women allow me to empower them to walk in the light."

Will you allow the Holy Spirit to empower you to walk in the light? You may already be experiencing some of the promptings of God's Spirit in this regard. Do you find yourself yearning for honest connection in the church where you worship? Are you tired of the superficiality that goes by the name of fellowship in your small group? Would you like to move beyond duplicity and deception in your relationships with your brothers and sisters in the faith? Do you long for real community in your local congregation? If your answer is yes to any of these questions, probably the Holy Spirit is stirring things up in you and seeking to draw you into a deeper shared life.

OVERCOMING OUR FEARS

The Holy Spirit draws us into a shared life by helping us overcome our fear of speaking about our lives with others. We live in a fear-filled atmosphere that infects our relationships with suspicion and reluctance. In addition, our individual fears stop us from opening ourselves to those whom God brings into our lives. Sadly, these fears, both from without and within, cause us to build big walls around our hearts. Small wonder we experience so much loneliness. Hearts that live behind fortresses of fear are always alienated hearts. If we wish to experience the gift of God's shared life among us, we need to be freed from these fears. The Holy Spirit does this by filling us with the love that God has for each of us. As the author of First John says later in his letter: "There is no fear in love. But perfect love drives out fear" (4:18).

I can vouch for this from personal experience. While I have always known theoretically that I need others if I want to grow in my relationship with God, I have constantly struggled with a fearful nervousness that comes from having an introverted and shy character. I find it quite scary to walk up to a group of people. Social occasions with strangers evoke great anxiety. It is far easier for me to be alone than with others. I often hesitate to express in company what I think and feel. So you will understand when I say that I have struggled over the years to open myself to the shared life that God wants us to experience. This fear has sometimes tempted me to withdraw from people and to keep my faith a private matter, even though I know that God does not do private salvation deals.

However, I have experienced inner shifts over the years. When I reflect on my journey with Christ, I see how his Spirit has helped me overcome many of my fears. This help has usually come through a vivid inner assurance of God's love for me. Overcoming my fear has brought wonderful benefits. Today I look back with much gratitude at all the gifts that have come to me through opening my life to other Christ-followers. Indeed, without the support, encouragement, and challenge of my brothers and sisters in the faith, I doubt whether I would still be traveling along the Jesus road.

Debbie and I meet every few weeks with seven young couples for three hours. It is a time of special sharing, mutual ministry, and quiet worship. Every time we drive home from this small group, we comment about the value of this time to us: the privilege of learning from a generation different from our own; the wonder of watching the Spirit at work in the lives of these young adults; the joy of having others pray with us when we struggle and fail. These are some of the amazing gifts that come our way when we allow the Spirit to help us overcome the fear of sharing our lives with one another within our faith community.

THREE COMMON FEARS

What fear keeps you from experiencing the shared life that God wants to give you? One fear I often hear voiced when I talk to folks about joining a small group is this: "I do not want to go off the deep end when it comes to my relationship with God." Many people fear they will become weird if they begin to take their faith seriously. They feel awkward about learning to pray in a group or studying the scriptures together or being open about their lives with others. They think this is for those odd types who have become "religious." I understand this fear. Many of us have given the Christian faith a bad reputation by the way we have related to others. But, as I often say to those I pastor, it is far more dangerous to dive into the shallow end than the deep end!

A second fear I regularly come across is that of being forced into certain ways of thinking and living. Again I can empathize. Not all spiritual groups are good at helping us share our lives. Some inhibit genuine fellowship through dogmatic leadership, legalistic attitudes, and conformist pressures. Consequently, such groups fail to create a safe, spacious, and sacred space for open self-disclosure and honest conversation. Perhaps you have experienced what I am describing, and you fear going through that again. I can only suggest that you let the Holy Spirit guide you to another group that respects and honors the freedom and dignity of each person who belongs. If you don't know of such a group, you may feel the Spirit's prompting to start a group where people can be themselves.

A third common fear I have encountered comes with the pressure of speaking in a group. This can be scary, especially when the expectation is that we will share information about ourselves or our relationship with God. Often we believe we don't have the right words or we won't say the right things or we won't have anything to say at all. This area is where so many have experienced the help of God's Spirit. This should not surprise us. Repeatedly in the Bible, the Holy Spirit gives people a fresh boldness or a new understanding to talk honestly about their experience of God or Christ in their lives. Paul may have had this in mind when he told Timothy that we have not been given a spirit of timidity but a spirit of "power, love and self-discipline" (2 Tim. 1:7).

We cannot grow in our relationship with God without others. To test out this statement, think for a moment about your circle of friends and acquaintances. I don't doubt that those growing in their discipleship and faith are those with significant connections to others. They worship with others on a regular basis, participate in smaller gatherings of Christ-followers, share their faith journeys with other companions along the way, and so on. In contrast, those who are stagnating in their relationship with God are most probably those who are trying to go it on their own. This is why I believe the Holy Spirit always wants to help us overcome our fear of opening ourselves to relationships with other people.

WIDENING OUR CIRCLE

The Holy Spirit draws us into a deeper shared life by widening our circle. I am sure that you have noticed the deep-seated human tendency to draw a circle around our lives. Usually we put people we like within our circle: those who agree with us, those who look like us, those who believe like us, those who worship like us, those who live like us. These are the people with whom we associate—get to know, give our time to, form friendships with. They are part of the "us," the ones with whom we share our lives, the people we include. Other people are part of "them," those whom we do not want to know, those whom we exclude. Sometimes we may even think that God prefers those who are inside our circles to those who are outside them.

When the Holy Spirit brings us alive to God's presence, the same Spirit challenges us to widen our circle. You can see this happening in the book of Acts after the Holy Spirit was poured out on

Jesus' early disciples. You will remember that they were Jews. One Jewish law concerned foods that could not be eaten. Nor were Jews allowed to associate with anyone who did eat these foods. Therefore, they were not allowed to enter the houses of Gentiles because Gentiles were unclean. Gentiles were not part of the Jewish circle. Imagine what an obstacle this presented to the spreading of the good news about Jesus! How could the gospel be brought to the non-Jewish world if those who were to carry the message could not associate with Gentiles?

We find the answer in the circle-widening work of the Holy Spirit in Peter's life. One day Peter went onto the roof of Simon the tanner to pray. He was hungry and was waiting for supper to be prepared. While he was praying, the Holy Spirit gave him a vision of a large sheet being lowered to earth from heaven. On it there were all kinds of four-footed animals, as well as reptiles and birds, including unclean creatures forbidden by Jewish law to be touched or eaten. Then Peter was told to get up, kill, and eat. Peter protested vehemently on the grounds that it was impure. Again the voice told him to eat, saying, "Do not call anything impure that God has made clean" (Acts 10:15). Such was Peter's stubbornness and prejudice that God had to speak three times to him. But this was not the end of the Holy Spirit's dealings with Peter on this matter. Stay with me for another paragraph!

Within moments of Peter awakening from his vision-experience, three Gentiles knocked on the door and asked for him. I like to call this a Holy Spirit coincidence. At that very moment, the Holy Spirit spoke again and told him that he must go with them. He invited them into the house, shared a meal with them, gave them a bed and then the next day accompanied them to Cornelius's home. There even more amazing things happened, but I will let you read about it for yourself. (Read the whole story in Acts 10:1-48.) It is an ongoing story of radical hospitality, profound humility, and astonishing miracles.

THE GREAT INCLUDER

This is how God widened Peter's circle and the circle of the early church to include Gentiles (non-Jewish people) in the Christian faith. Peter's main lesson about the Holy Spirit was this: The Spirit of Christ is the Great Includer who continually seeks to widen our circles. This means embracing those different from us, listening to their stories, and becoming friends in the process. When we start to follow him, Jesus brings people into our lives who may differ greatly from us.

As I reflect on my own journey with God, I see how the Spirit has been doing this in my life up to this present moment. As a Christ-follower, my earliest fellowship circle was quite small. It was made up of people very much like me—white, English, Methodist, middle-class, heterosexual, able-bodied, and so on. However, over the years, I have experienced the circle-widening work of the Holy Spirit in many ways. Along the way I have had to face up to my prejudices, confront the smallness of my heart and my thinking, learn to listen and rethink many of my naïve assumptions about those who differ from me in terms of race, class, doctrine, sexual orientation, and outlook on life. The resulting shared life transcends the external characteristics that often keep us apart.

Let me relate one personal example from my early days as a Christ-follower. In the late seventies I met Lulamile, a colleague in ministry who was a little older than me. We came from completely different worlds within the same country. I had grown up with the privileges that came with being white in apartheid South Africa. He had grown up within the context of oppression, painful discrimination, and economic poverty that went with being black in apartheid South Africa. In a country designed to separate us, we gradually became close friends. We spent many hours together, talking into the late hours of the night; experienced each other's worlds; shared our different views and somehow always stayed connected even in moments of disagreement and misunderstanding. This one friendship introduced me to the wider community from which he came. Debbie and I experienced an incredibly special moment when he joined us together as marriage partners. Today as I look back, I see this widening of my circle as a critical part of the work of the Holy Spirit in my life.

Perhaps you can reflect on how the Holy Spirit is encouraging you right now to draw your circle wider. This is not an easy journey. Peter in the book of Acts found it a difficult journey, and it will be for us too. Not only are our lives often turned upside down by these encounters, sometimes those who live in a small circle find it hard to relate to us when our circle grows bigger. The most attacking e-mails and calls that I have received over the years have been from brothers and sisters in the faith who have been unhappy with some of the company I keep. But the Holy Spirit insistently challenges us to recognize that God is actively at work in the lives of those we keep outside our small circle. You and I need to acknowledge this activity and then build into our lives a practice that aligns our hearts with the heartbeat of the Spirit. We now explore one such practice.

TAKING AN INTEREST IN OTHERS

I want to explore the simple, everyday practice of taking an interest in others. It is one of the greatest gifts we can give to those around us, especially those who feel excluded. We are surrounded by people who, even though they live and work in big cities and suburbs, feel alienated from those around them. This alienation happens in our places of work, our church communities, and even our homes. People can be colleagues for years or sit next to each other in the pews week after week or be in a marriage for years and never truly connect. Can you see the healing and life-giving value of a genuine attempt to reach out to someone like this?

The first step in taking an interest in others begins when we realize the immense human and spiritual value of such a practice. The practice moves us out of our self-preoccupied, self-absorbed worlds into the worlds of others. We discover that beneath our external and superficial differences, human beings have many feelings and traits in common: our deep longing for intimacy, our joys and sorrows, our hopes and dreams for a better future for ourselves and our children. When we begin to communicate with one another at this level, we open our hearts and lives more widely to the shared life God wants us to experience. Paul challenges us to look not "to your own interests but each of you to the interests of the others" (Phil. 2:4).

The second step is to look outward and actually *see* the other person whom God may want us to move toward. In order to notice others, we must be aware enough to look outside ourselves. We must open our eyes to see beyond ourselves, our circle of friends, our interests and desires. Frequently when we are in a big group, we gravitate to our own friends and start talking about our common interests. How seldom do we pause, look around, and ask ourselves, *I wonder if there is someone here who is new or lonely, a person who needs me to take an interest in him or her?*

The third step comes in reaching out and making an effort to connect. This can be difficult for those who are more introverted. But as we saw earlier, the Holy Spirit helps us. Here are some simple questions that when asked respectfully and courteously can help us begin a conversation. *Where are you from? What brings you here? Do you have family?* Asking such questions after we have introduced ourselves can open up conversation. We then simply listen in an interested way to the other person's responses. We can easily pose a question and then begin answering it from our own perspective! But asking some of the above questions and taking an interest in the other person's responses can lead to further questions so that both people experience the shared life of the Spirit.

If we consciously build it into our lives, gradually this practice can begin to change the persons we are and the way we relate to others. We do not simply add this practice onto our lives. *We become persons who are interested in others.* We live in the continuous current of the Holy Spirit. The love of God pours into our lives and through us into the lives of others. We give up our self-centered ways of living and discover that we are made for community. We start to live beyond loneliness and help others to do so as well. We relate to others in a flesh-and-blood way, giving to them and receiving from them. We experience the shared life that the Holy Spirit gives us, with the Father and the Son and with one another. We participate in God's good-news story. Our joy is made complete.

SMALL-GROUP CONVERSATION STARTERS

Icebreaker: Share a memory from the first church to which you belonged.

1. How do you feel about sharing in a small group?
2. Why do you think we find it hard to be honest about our lives with others in the church?
3. Name one fear that sometimes keeps you from full participation in small-group life with other Christ-followers.
4. Share one example from your own life where the Holy Spirit has widened your circle to include someone you had previously excluded.
5. How could you become more intentional in looking toward the interests of others?

FOUR

THE GIFT GOD GIVES
. . . Transforms Us Inwardly

Writing about how the Holy Spirit changes us inwardly is rather daunting. I feel like Gandhi must have felt when a troubled mother brought her daughter to see him about her addiction to sweets. The story goes that he asked the mother to bring her daughter back in three weeks. The mother went away and returned after three weeks. This time the spiritual master took the young girl aside and explained to her in a few simple words the harmful effects of eating too many sweets. Thanking Gandhi for giving her daughter such good advice, the mother then asked him, "But I would like to know why you did not say those words to my daughter three weeks ago when I first brought her to you." He replied, "Three weeks ago I was still addicted to eating sweet foods myself!"[1]

Even though I have been following Jesus for over four decades, so much change still needs to take place inside me. I often find myself longing to be a better person. I long to be more caring and loving toward those close to me, more courageous when it comes to standing for what is good and beautiful and true, more responsive to the incredible depths of human suffering that surround us, freer from attachments that I know keep me from becoming the person God wants me to be. Can you see why I feel a little like Gandhi did when that mother asked him to help her daughter? A huge part of me believes I need to experience far more change myself before I write about it.

The challenge of writing this chapter becomes even more daunting when we consider the kind of inner change we are considering. We are not referring to what some may call self-help or self-improvement programs. Helpful as these may be, these programs usually focus on external changes in behavior that come about through insight and trying harder. The changes that the Holy Spirit brings about are radically different. Although they may certainly involve both insight and effort on our part, resulting in new patterns of behavior, they go beyond them. The roots of genuine spiritual transformation lie in those parts of the human heart and mind that only the Holy Spirit can touch.

So at the outset let me clarify the kind of change God's Spirit wants to make in us. I will state it as simply as I can and later unpack it more fully: *The Holy Spirit wants to change you and me into a "little Christ."*[2]

IS IT REALLY POSSIBLE?

The blunt statement above may surprise you. We think that because Jesus was God's unique Son, we can never become like him. By contrast, those who wrote the New Testament saw things differently. They believed that God wants us to share in the divine life of Christ and become like him. One of my favorite Bible verses comes in Paul's letter to the Corinthians where he writes the following: "And we all, who with unveiled faces contemplate the Lord's glory, are being transformed into his image with ever-increasing glory, which comes from the Lord, who is the Spirit" (2 Cor. 3:18).

Let me repeat that this inward change brought about by the Spirit differs from the self-help and self-improvement kind. Here we are looking at a much deeper, much bigger, and certainly more radical change. The Spirit's change brings about a transformed sense of identity. We find our personalities being totally renovated from the inside. We respond to others with a new seeing, a new listening, and a new heart. We begin living with a fresh awareness of God's presence in and around us. When Christ enters our lives, he does not want to *improve* us; he wants to *change* us. Conversion, which we looked at in a previous chapter, is a process of inner change that lasts a lifetime.

We need to grasp this deeper, bigger, and more radical way of speaking about inner change. Failure to do so will lead us into a smug satisfaction with the status quo of our outwardly respectable lives or into some deadly form of external legalism or fatalistic resignation that we will always be like we are. When this happens, we hold a superficial understanding of how God wants to change us. Many who live at this surface level never get to experience the Christ-life that the Holy Spirit offers us. We may find ourselves "born again," but we fail to learn to live again in a new way.

What is your response to the possibility of becoming a "little Christ"? Perhaps you feel this option exists for others who are more "spiritual" than you. Or maybe you think that it is an idealistic goal and totally inaccessible to ordinary people like yourself. Or does it sound as if it will take all the fun out of your life? Or you may have no idea even how to go about it. In my walk with Jesus, I have wrestled with each of these responses in one way or another. Some aspects have become clearer to me. Let me share some of these discoveries with you. I hope they will help you open yourself to the divine intimacy and radical love that the Holy Spirit wants to bring in your life and in mine.

BECOMING A LITTLE CHRIST

I heard a delightful story the other day. A father was making pancakes for his two young sons. The sons began arguing about who would get the first pancake. Dad thought this was a good moment to teach his boys a gospel lesson. "If Jesus were here with us now," he explained to them, "he would let his brother have the first pancake." The two children grew quiet as they thought about their father's words. After a while the older brother said to his sibling, "Okay, then, you can be Jesus today."

What does it mean in practical terms for you and me to become a little Christ? Let me first clarify what it *does not mean.* It does not mean trying to copy the Palestinian life of the historical Jesus. He did not live in the twenty-first century, travel on congested highways, have to answer e-mails, have a wife and children, and perform all the tasks that you and I face on a daily basis. We cannot imitate the external details of Jesus' life within the context of our lives today. Imagine, for a moment, wearing sandals and robes to work, walking from home to work, washing one another's feet at mealtimes!

Becoming a little Christ centers on becoming more like Christ in heart and mind. This process of becoming does not involve unfathomable mystery. We catch glimpses of what it entails as we trace the footsteps of Jesus through the Gospels, meditate on his teachings about the good life, observe his ministry encounters with hurting women and men, and watch him embrace the injustice of unfair condemnation and dying on a cross as a common criminal. As we read the four Gospels with these things in mind, we come to know what Jesus was really like and what it would mean for the Holy Spirit to form Jesus' heart and mind in us.

JESUS IN HIS GOSPEL LIFE

As I have tried to get to know Jesus better through his Gospel life, several of his characteristics have struck me powerfully.[3] First of all, throughout his earthly life Jesus remains his own person. He is the same person inside and out; he never wears masks and is always his true self. Because he knows himself as God's beloved Son, he is radically free to be himself. His wonderfully authentic life in the Gospels frees us from any kind of carbon copy Christianity. When Christ enters our lives, his Spirit wants to free us to become the unique persons God desires that we be.

The second characteristic that I noticed was the incredibly loving way that Jesus relates to people. People matter to him. He acknowledges the sacred worth of God in every person, especially in those who have been written off as inferior, worthless, or unacceptable. Whether he is hugging a little child, touching a rejected leper, being politically incorrect by sitting down for a meal with a tax collector, showing acceptance to a used and abused prostitute, or considering his mother's future while he hangs on the cross, Jesus treats people with immeasurable respect and thoughtful care. His love and compassion convey to the persons he meets the realization that they too are God's beloved.

The third outstanding feature of Jesus' life is his radical confidence in the God whom he experiences intimately as his Abba Father and whose will is his dearest passion. This loving union between Jesus and his Father is the fervent center of his life. Jesus says only what the Father wants him to say. He does only what he sees the Father doing. His primary concern centers on the Father's desires. (See John 5:19; 10:37; 14:24.) From Jesus' unique oneness with his heavenly Father he derives the insight, the strength, and the power to fulfill his calling as the Servant-Messiah in God's purposes for humanity. Indeed, we cannot understand his life apart from this divine intimacy and single-minded obedience to his Father's will.

This brief reflection on Jesus' life offers a few clues about what it means practically for the Holy Spirit to form Christ in us. At the very least, this journey will have three interconnected dimensions: It will be a journey in which the Holy Spirit helps us to unmask the many levels of pretense in our lives and become more truly ourselves. It is a journey in which the Holy Spirit helps us to move away from self-absorption and give ourselves more lovingly to those around us. It is a journey in which the Holy Spirit helps us yield ourselves more generously to God's dream for a Christ-healed world. This is what is involved in the Holy Spirit's enabling you and me to become little Christs.

When the Holy Spirit fills our lives and Christ is being formed within, it is impossible to conceal it. We become increasingly real, open, and honest. Those closest to us feel deeply loved. We respond to those who suffer, especially our nearest neighbor. Joy bubbles out of us. Peace and serenity shine through us. We remain hopeful in all circumstances. We fall in love with God. We are aware and responsive to God's presence. We thirst for God's reign in our lives, communities, and world. All this and more marks the life of one being changed inwardly by the Spirit of Christ. Many of us have known persons like this, and the radiant impression they leave stays with us for many years.

THE LONG JOURNEY INVOLVED

As I mentioned earlier, my moments of inconsistency and failure make me feel uneasy writing about inner change. With all my heart I want the Holy Spirit to form Christ within me. I desire to become more truly the person God wants me to be. I want to love and care for those I encounter every day, especially those closest to me and those in pain. I want desperately to live with a more intimate and continuing awareness of God's presence in and around my life. Yet, if I am honest, I must say that who I am and who I want to be and what happens in my life are often far apart from one another.

I shall relate an incident that occurred while I was writing this chapter. The other evening I went to buy a takeout meal for Debbie and me. While I was waiting for my spicy chicken meal, a man selling belts approached me. We introduced ourselves and got into a conversation. It had been a futile day trying to sell his merchandise, and he was feeling quite despondent. He then asked me if I had any money for him. I said that I only had a credit card on me. It was untrue. I had some money in my pocket. In spite of everything I have written above about wanting Christ to be formed in my life, I still did not speak the truth in this encounter.

Later that evening as I thought about this encounter, it became clearer to me that this deception reflected a deeper pattern of dishonesty in my life when it comes to my relationships with those in desperate economic need. Why was I not honest with him? Why had I been so reluctant to experience the discomfort of saying that I did have money in my pocket but did not want to give it to him? I have been thinking about this matter quite a lot since this incident took place. But the point that I want to make here is this: Despite my desire for inward change by the Holy Spirit into Christ-likeness, I still mess up and sin in embarrassing ways.

Thankfully, New Testament writers use words and images that suggest this process of inner change is a journey we go on with the Holy Spirit. We begin as "babes in Christ" when we invite the risen Jesus into our lives. As the Spirit of Christ starts to transform our lives, we gradually mature and grow up into Christ. The Holy Spirit does not change us instantaneously. Inner transformation is a long, unfolding process, though it may well have some decisive moments within it. The journey continues into eternity. We can never say that we have arrived. We are always pilgrims on the way toward becoming little Christs. (See 1 Cor. 3:1; 13:9, 12 and 2 Cor. 3:18; 4:16.)

I have also learned from my own experience, from the experience of other Christ-followers, and from the experiences of God's people in God's good-news story that this journey is not a straight line. We do not go directly from being a babe in Christ to being mature in Christ. More often than not, it seems like we take three steps forward and two back. The journey seems erratic, much more like a roller-coaster ride than a trip up an escalator. One moment we respond maturely in a difficult situation, and the goodness of Christ shines through us. The next moment we respond childishly and wonder whether Christ is in our lives at all. This is what happened for me outside the fast food outlet where I waited for my takeout chicken. Within a second I had fallen back into old patterns of deception and let myself down, as well as the God whom I love so much.

The erratic nature of the journey requires patience and perseverance. I appreciate the story of the peasant woman who passed by a monk while walking in the village street. She fell prostrate before him and asked him, "Please tell me, holy father, what do you men of God do up there in the monastery on the hill? It appears that you are so close to heaven. How do you spend your time and hours?" The humble and wise monk responded simply. "What do we do up there in the monastery so close to heaven? I will tell you. We fall down and we get up! We fall down and get up! We fall down and get up!"[4] How typically this pattern mirrors the transforming journey we undertake when we become Christ-followers.

INNER CHANGE IS AN INSIDE JOB

At the risk of tediously repeating myself, let me again describe the inner change God wants to bring about in our lives. We need clarity before taking our next step. The inner change does not involve copying Jesus in the external details of his life. Reflecting Christ in our daily lives means growing into the special and unique persons God wants us to be. It means becoming permeated by the God-love that we see in Jesus for all people. It means coming to know Abba Father as intimately and confidently as Jesus did. Pulling these three clues together, it is all about letting the Holy Spirit change you and me inwardly into little Christs.

How then does this inner change take place? The New Testament answer to this question has two sides. On one side, we clearly understand that the Holy Spirit changes us. As we turn toward Christ and entrust ourselves to him in conversion, his Spirit comes to live within us in a new way. To experience the inner change that God wants to bring about within us, we need to remain open to God's Spirit. Only the loving action of the Holy Spirit transforms us into our true selves, permeated by the love that we see in Jesus and deepened in our consciousness of God's presence in our lives. Real change is always an inside work of the Spirit, a transforming gift of grace to those who live with open hands before God—never a human achievement that we bring about on our own.

I stress this point. Often when I preach and teach about these matters, someone will say to me afterward, "Thank-you for your words. I am going to try harder to be a little Christ." This response is not surprising. We live in a day and age characterized by self-help and self-improvement mind-sets, which have infiltrated the church as well. Think about some recent sermons that you have heard. How many of them have assumed that you can change if you just try hard enough? Somehow we tend to believe that by our own unaided effort we can make ourselves become like Jesus.

We will fail time and time again in this impossible undertaking. If we continue down this path, we end up in a place of extreme disillusionment, spiritual weariness, and paralyzing discouragement. Effort alone does not work. We can become so negative that we lose all motivation to change. "Count me out," we may hear ourselves saying to other Christ-followers. "All this talk about becoming a little Christ may well have been the goal of those saints with a halo around their heads, but it is certainly not possible for an ordinary person like me."

BUT WE MUST COOPERATE

But we must also avoid the opposite error of assuming that we can do *nothing*. Inner change does not just happen. It is not automatic. It is a work of the Holy Spirit with which we cooperate. Hence the other side of our answer must affirm our part in the journey toward transformation. Faith without action is dead. The spiritual journey demands thoughtful effort. Personal change requires our determined, intentional, and planned participation. We work with the Spirit to become all that God intends us to be. Compassion is not for the lazy and passive. Our connection with God deepens only as we take appropriate measures to open our lives to the Holy Spirit.

We cannot neglect this side of the conversion journey. Sometimes we think to ourselves that if we have the right spiritual experience, we can sit back and let God do the rest. Living in an instant society where everything must happen now encourages this outlook. This belief has many people searching for the latest spiritual experience in the hope that God will change them instantaneously by "zapping" them with the Spirit from heaven. Before the worship service is over, they want to be completely new people. "Come up to the front of the church," we hear the pastor say, "and let the Holy Spirit change you right now."

Genuine inner change does not happen in this fashion. We know this from both personal experience and observation. Consider someone who has struggled since childhood with an explosive temper. It constantly expresses itself in things like road rage, foul language, and outbursts of angry words. One Sunday at church the preacher's sermon states that only the Holy Spirit can change us.

The man realizes that God is speaking to him. After the sermon, he kneels at the altar rail and asks for ministry. Someone prays for him and invites the Holy Spirit to come upon him and make him a new person. While this experience may cause a huge shift in his relationship with God, it is highly unlikely that from that moment on he will not struggle with his temper again.

This is why I describe a practice at the end of each chapter. Each one is a simple, down-to-earth way in which we cooperate with the Holy Spirit in the conversion of our lives. I like the way Paul describes this tension between what God does and what we must do in this transformative journey. Writing to the Philippians, he urges them to "continue to work out your salvation with fear and trembling, for it is God who works in you to will and to act in order to fulfill his good purpose" (2:12-13). All the practices that I describe in this book play an important role in opening our lives more widely and more deeply to the Holy Spirit. I find one practice especially relevant to this chapter's theme, and we now turn to it.

RECEIVING PRAYER

Broadly speaking, when it comes to the landscape of prayer, we can identify two kinds of praying: giving prayer and receiving prayer. In giving prayer we bring to God our praise, our thankfulness, our confession, our intercessions, our needs and concerns, and so on. We talk with God and ask for what we need. Receiving prayer is a quieter, more restful and silent way of praying. I want to suggest that the regular practice of this second kind of praying helps us cooperate with the Holy Spirit in the transformation of our lives.[5]

Remember what I stated about the Holy Spirit in the first chapter. Through the Holy Spirit, God is constantly giving God's self in love and grace to us in the here and now. Whenever we experience in fuller measure these divine twins, God's love and grace, the Spirit changes us a little bit more. But, as we have noted, love and grace do not drop on our heads from heaven. We must intentionally receive them. Only then do they begin to change us inwardly. Over the centuries Christ-followers have found that taking time for receiving prayer on a regular basis enables this inward receiving.

These two ways of praying—giving prayer and receiving prayer—correspond closely to two basic needs of human relationship. In any healthy relationship we need both to give and to receive. We need to give love and to receive love. We need to give trust and to receive trust. We need to give attention and to receive attention. In our close relationships, the receiving and the giving intermingle. At times we may be more aware of one than the other. But both aspects need to be present for our relationships to grow and mature. If only one is present, the relationship ends up being lopsided.

Relationship with our Abba Father requires that we learn how to give and receive in prayer. Often we fuse these two ways of praying in our experience of prayer. I have a hunch that we feel more at home with the first kind of prayer than the second. My earliest teachers in the faith helped me tremendously in the talking part of my praying but not so much with the receiving part. Over recent years it has been good to discover how to receive love and grace from God and to experience more deeply the Holy Spirit's transforming presence in my life.

All of us have to consider how best to pray in this way, but let me tell you how I am learning to receive in prayer. Most mornings I arrive at my office about an hour before I start working. I begin my time of prayer by relaxing into God's presence. I normally sit— quiet, relaxed—remembering God's presence within me and around me. I ask the Holy Spirit to help me be open to the love and grace that comes to me each moment from God's heart. Sometimes a few items weigh so heavily on my mind that I blurt them out immediately to God, but talking with God is not the main purpose of this time together. Receiving prayer for me is more about creating space for the Holy Spirit to work in me. I embrace other times when I can speak at length with God.

Once I have settled into the quiet, I read a few words from God's good-news story in scripture. I usually have chosen a Bible passage before beginning my time of prayer. I am not trying to learn anything new while I read; rather, I am seeking to meet with God. It is like slowly reading a letter from my wife, Debbie. As I read, I begin to think of her. The letter helps me feel closer to her, and often I can sense my own love for her deepening. Most of all, savoring the letter renews my sense of Debbie's love for me. Her words on paper help me receive her love into my life. I have this same experience when I read a scripture passage slowly. It helps me refocus on those warm rays of divine love and grace that God continuously sends out.

Next, I receive God's love and grace into my life by opening my heart and mind to God. This is the way I approach it: I have a favorite love-word for God. I whisper it over and over again as an expression of my love for God. Sometimes I will use the phrase, "Lord Jesus Christ, have mercy on me." At other times I express no words, only the longing of my heart to know Christ more deeply. Then I sit in the silence with God with my hands open. Obviously, distracting thoughts jostle around in my mind and clamor for my attention. I don't get too worried about this and have learned to let these thoughts go as they come. Then I return to my love-word for God or to my prayer for Jesus' mercy or to my deep longings. This silent part of my praying forms the longest part of my time of receiving prayer.

Finally, when it is time to end my time of prayer, my thoughts turn outward. So I hold each person in my family and one or two others in my heart before God—people I know who are going through a difficult time and who need my prayer and care. I also think of the day ahead and ask for God's guidance in whatever practical tasks I am facing. Sometimes at the end of this time with

God I record in my journal the activities I need to pursue—an e-mail to answer, a telephone call to make, a text message to send, a difficult situation to face, an apology to make. These practical things that I intend to do express my personal response to God's love and grace in down-to-earth ways.

I trust that I have whetted your appetite to explore what receiving prayer might look like in your life. There is no single way to do this. Each of us needs to find his or her own way. As we do, we rest assured that the Holy Spirit is at work in the hidden depths of our beings and will teach us along the way. We need not worry too much or be too introspective. As one of my friends once told me, "Trevor, if you plant potatoes, you do not constantly dig up the soil to see if they are growing or not. You water the ground regularly and then trust that the potatoes will grow as they should." It is the same with receiving prayer. We open ourselves to God's love and grace and trust that the Holy Spirit will gradually change us into little Christs in the midst of our everyday lives.

SMALL-GROUP CONVERSATION STARTERS

Icebreaker: When you were a child, what got you into the most trouble with your parents?

1. In what one way would you most like to experience inner change?
2. How do you respond to the possibility of becoming a little Christ?
3. What about the gospel life of Jesus attracts you the most?
4. How do you respond to the idea that the Holy Spirit brings about inner change?
5. What do you think about the idea of "receiving prayer"?

FIVE

THE GIFT GOD GIVES
. . . Guides Us in Our Decision Making

Yesterday I spent time with a businessman who wanted to talk. When I asked why he had come, he said that since his recent conversion he wanted to do whatever God wanted him to do; but he was struggling with a painful business dilemma. As the owner of a medium-sized manufacturing company, he employed about forty people. The last year had been tough. Now he was trying to decide whether God wanted him to restructure and downsize or to press on with his present staff complement. The first option would mean retrenching a number of staff, many of whom were breadwinners. The second was financially risky given the bleak outlook for his industry in the coming year. He hoped our time together would help him to make a faithful decision.

As a pastor I often spend time with people who want to make good, wise, and sensible decisions. Usually they are sincere men and women who have come alive to God's presence in their lives, who are on a journey with Jesus Christ, and who now want to discern and do God's will. They have found a new direction for their lives. They want to praise, love, and serve God. They know that they must not do wrong and avoid doing anything stupid. However, we all know that a wide range of choices exists between these two general guidelines. Rather than making unwise choices, these people desire to do that which will most resonate with the heart of God.

I am sure you can identify with this. Each day we make decisions. Sometimes they are big ones involving careers, business options, significant relationships, and finances. Then we face those many smaller ones about how to spend our time, how to respond in conflict decisions, what to give attention to, and what to put off for another day. Our responses shape our lives; we become the persons we are through the decisions we make. So we ask questions like these: How do we find God's way for our lives? How do we make choices that are in tune with God's purposes? How can we know when God is speaking to us? How do we help each other with these questions?

These questions deserve careful thought because persons in authority can easily abuse their power. Think for a moment of some religious leaders who claim a special hotline to God. They confidently assert God's speaking to them and impose these revelations on their followers. These religious leaders then expect members of their communities to toe the line, uncritically support their leaders, and follow through without question. Sometimes this abuse can occur on a personal level as well. The other day I spoke with a young adult whose small-group leader in a nearby megachurch had said to him, "The Spirit has instructed me to tell you to end the relationship with your girlfriend immediately."

We give careful thought to these matters for other reasons as well. Some people genuinely believe that God does not speak to them. You may be one of these. Perhaps you feel that you are too insignificant to garner God's interest in your activities. Early in my walk with God I was not entirely convinced that God wanted to guide me in my daily decision making. Yes, I did believe that God had given general guidelines in the Bible about how to order our lives. But when it came to those decisions that the Bible did not specifically cover (like where to live or how to manage my time or what to preach on), I did not actually believe that God would personally lead me.

Today I view things differently. Let me explain why. Throughout God's good-news story in the Bible, we come across the theme of the Holy Spirit as guide. Here are a few examples. In the Old Testament the Spirit constantly guides the people of Israel in many ways, including through dreams, visions, voices, and signs. (See passages like 1 Sam. 3:15; Dan. 2:19; 1 Kings 19:11-13.) In the Gospels we read that the Spirit "drove" Jesus into the desert. (See Matt. 4:1; Mark 1:12; Luke 4:1.) As followers of Christ, Paul tells us that we are now no longer under law but rather led by the Spirit. (See Rom. 8:14; Gal. 5:18.) In the book of Acts we note the early church's guidance by the Spirit. (See passages like Acts 8:29; 10:19; 13:2; 15:28; 16:7; 21:4.) Biblical references like these encourage us to believe that the Spirit's guidance covers all kinds of decisions. Indeed, in light of this strong biblical support for God's guidance, we can affirm boldly this bit of good news: *The Holy Spirit wants to guide us in our decision making.*

However, this bold statement leaves us with the practical question, "How does the Holy Spirit guide us?" In the rest of this chapter, I will impart some thoughts that have helped me as I have sought the Spirit's guidance for my life.

GUIDES US IN FREEDOM

When I spend time with young people who are exploring God's guidance, one issue always comes up. It usually goes like this: How will I know when I have met the person God wants me to marry? The question triggers much nervous anxiety. I can understand why. What happens if we misread God's signals about who this person is? What if we marry the wrong person? Are we then stepping out of God's will for our lives? Will God bless our marriage if we make the wrong decision? If you are married and reading this, even now you may be wondering whether you did the right thing in marrying the person you did! Issues like this raise difficult questions around the will of God, which we need to address if we want to explore how the Spirit guides us.

Sometimes we talk about the will of God as though it were some heavenly blueprint for our lives. According to this way of thinking, if we want to do God's will, we need to get in touch with this fixed celestial blueprint and then apply it to the different situations of our lives. Someone said to me the other day, as we sat talking together after a service, "How do I download God's computer printout for my future?" Thinking about God's guidance in this way can often lead to inner distress and anxiety, especially if we end up making decisions that do not seem to be going well. For this reason, I find this particular approach unhelpful. However, allow me to voice another concern.

I believe this approach severely limits the precious gift of freedom that God has given each of us. God's good-news story indicates that God created us to live as free human beings. Recall the first three chapters of Genesis. There we see that God wants us to be free to shape our lives and our world through our choices. The only stipulation is that we not take over God's role. Now the idea of trying to apply an *exact* blueprint for our lives severely undermines this freedom. As one writer, commenting on this understanding of God's will, puts it: "The scope of our freedom is reduced to choosing to fit in, whether we like it or not, with what God has 'planned' for us, once we think we know what it is."[1] It goes without saying that this is very little freedom indeed.

Let me describe a much more positive understanding of God's will for our lives. Rather than anxiously trying to work out the heavenly blueprint, we could say that doing God's will is more about learning how to think and act as God would if God were in our situation—which does not mean that anything goes! God has given us guidelines to help us exercise this freedom responsibly in making our decisions: the gift of scripture, the gift of counsel from our faith-family in Christ from the time of Acts into the present, the gift of our own reasoning and imagining abilities, and also the gift of our own conscience. Through these gifts the Holy Spirit influences our thinking and our perspective. But in the end we have to choose to do what we honestly believe to be most in tune with God's heart. When we follow this approach, we could say that God wants us to *improvise* freely the will of God in our lives.

IMPROVISING THE WILL OF GOD

Before I go any farther, let me state what I mean when I use the word *improvise*. Improvisation, as you know, comes from the theater world. Through this practice, actors develop trust in who they are and trust in one another so they may conduct unscripted dramas without fear.[2] When I write about our improvising the will of God within our lives, I mean to think and act as we believe God would think and act if God were in our situation, especially in those situations not covered in the Bible. I will stress again that when we do this, we do not start from scratch. We have been given the drama of God's good-news story in scriptures. Also, as those who follow Christ, we are part of a community that has sought to do this since biblical times. In our task of improvisation, we can learn from these fellow Christ-followers of the past and the present.

Let me offer an illustration that may help us better understand what it means to improvise God's will in our lives.[3] Suppose we found an incomplete play by William Shakespeare. Let's say that we discovered the first four acts and the last act. How do we go about performing the play? Obviously, we are not Shakespeare and we cannot write as well as he could. So what can we do? Well, we could search out some people who really appreciate Shakespeare and give the play to them. They would then immerse themselves in the five acts that we do have. We could talk about it together and then imagine how we would perform the missing act as best we can. This improvisation would look different each time the play was performed, but always it would seek to be faithful to the spirit of Shakespeare. Do you not think that Shakespeare would be pleased with our efforts at improvisation? We are trying to think and act as he would if he were in our situation.

In the same way, we can say that we have in our possession the unfinished drama of God's good-news story. We have the first four acts—the first being the story of Creation and the tragic fall of humankind; the second being the experiences of the people of Israel; the third act remembering Jesus' life, death, resurrection and ascension; and the fourth focusing on the gift of the Spirit and the beginnings of the early church. These four acts are complete as far as they go, but our story is missing. We have the final act in the book of Revelation, which describes the victory of Christ over evil and the coming of God's new heaven and new earth. But God has given us powers of thought and imagination, as well as the ability to envision how to go about writing and performing the missing act. God has also given us the gift of one another for this task.

How then do we go about this improvisation? We read about God's good-news story as told in scripture over and over again. There we catch a glimpse of God's love for us and of God's dream for the world. We discover God's desire to be in intimate relationship with us, and we get to know God's character, especially as we see it reflected in Jesus. We find out what gives God joy and what breaks God's heart. We see how the earliest followers of Jesus implemented God's dream within the challenges of their first-century world. The list of things we would learn from immersing ourselves in God's good-news story goes on and on. We would talk about our learnings with those friends who also want to do God's will in their lives. Then we use our common sense. We take seriously the voice of our consciences and, as best as we can, we go ahead and freely improvise the missing act of God's good-news story for our lives and for our time. We would write our story and live it out with all the faith, hope, and love that we have.

You may be wondering where the Holy Spirit is in all this. We have a great advantage over the Shakespearian actors. As we move ahead to write the missing act of our story in God's good-news story, the Spirit of the Great Author resides with us. Remember one of the key points from the first chapter: The Holy Spirit is God with us today, alive in the here and now, present with you and me, right now. In our efforts at improvisation, we have the wonderful privilege of being able to check with the Author as to whether we are on the right track! How the Holy Spirit guides us is the focus of the next section. At this point things really get creative, risky, and challenging. Keep reading!

GUIDES US IN PEACE

In one respect there is no great mystery surrounding the will of God. Generally speaking, we all know what God wants. We all know that God wants us to love, to be honest, to serve others, to use our gifts, and to do as much good as we can. We know these things from understanding the five acts of God's Love Story that we have. What we still need to discern, however, is *how* to do these things. In what ways are we to love those around us, be truthful, serve others, use our gifts, and do the good within the specific situations of our everyday lives? It is not just a case of choosing between right and wrong. Rather, it is all about learning how best to improvise the personal will of God in our story. Thankfully, we are not left on our own to work this out. The Holy Spirit is with us, wanting to guide us in the decisions we have to make, right where we are.

Let me describe one way this happens. It is a way suggested by scripture and confirmed in the testimony of countless Christ-followers through the centuries. This way helps us to realize that God guides ordinary people like you and me. It takes seriously the living and active presence of the Holy Spirit in everything that takes place within and around us. It affirms strongly that God's Spirit communicates with us through the deep inner movements of our heart. It is accessible to all of us, no matter who we are, whether we are mature Christ-followers or just beginning the journey. In a nutshell, this way involves paying close attention to the different feelings that our thinking about possible decisions grants us. Here is how it works.

When we think about making a decision that is in sync with God's personal will for our lives, the Holy Spirit will give us a sense of deep peace. By the word *peace* I do not mean a superficial sense of pleasure or feeling good or merely being happy. Rather, I mean a profound sense of well-being and aliveness that comes from being in harmony with God's desires for our lives. I feel sure that you know what I am trying to describe. Even when we believe that God wants us to travel down a painful or difficult road and we feel quite scared and nervous, we experience God's peace within us that nothing can take away. Such a feeling indicates that we are on the right path for our lives. It leads us to feel calm, confident, and encouraged in whatever decision we think we must make.

Many Bible passages encourage us along this path of discerning God's guidance. Consider the time when Paul writes to the Colossians, encouraging them to allow the peace of Christ to guide them in their decision making. (See Col. 3:15.) In another interesting moment, Paul explains to the Corinthians his decision to follow the leading of the Spirit:

> When I went to Troas to preach the gospel of Christ and found that the Lord had opened a door for me, I still had no peace of mind, because I did not find my brother Titus there. So I said goodbye to them and went on to Macedonia (2 Cor. 2:12).

Notice that only having an open door of opportunity was not enough to guide Paul in action. He also needed a strong inner sense of peace and rightness within.

On the other hand, sensing unease and disquiet about taking an action might cause us to pause and reconsider. Feelings like these are the opposite of the peaceful ones that accompany decisions that are in tune with God. Instead, we somehow feel at odds with God. We experience ourselves as being out of sync with what God wants. Sometimes these negative feelings arise even when the decision, on the surface, looks beneficial to us. These feelings can signal the Holy Spirit's nudging us to think more carefully about the decision facing us. In recent years I have learned not to move forward with decisions that I feel unsettled about. Rather, I continue to think and pray about alternatives until God's Spirit leads me with the peace that I have tried to describe above.

THE DANGER OF A FALSE PEACE

Obviously we need to watch out for a false sense of peace, which may have several sources. It can come from wanting to escape a conflict-ridden situation, from trying to avoid some necessary suffering, from not wanting to move out of a comfortable and familiar place. False peace may be superficial and temporary, offering quick relief when facing difficult choices. The peace given by God's Spirit endures through all the ups and downs of our more fleeting emotions and moods. It does not mean the absence of trouble. Rather, it means a strong conviction, even in the midst of conflict, that God is with us and we are not alone. For this reason an inner joy, aliveness, and serenity often accompany the peace given by the Holy Spirit—no matter what is happening around us.

Being led by the Holy Spirit in this way does not mean that everything works out perfectly. Sometimes we believe that if we follow God's leading and do what God wants us to do, we will experience no negative consequences. Then when conflict arises, we wonder whether we have made the right decision. For example, someone believes that God led him to accept a certain job. One day he begins to experience discord at work. If this person believes that everything should be perfect when God leads us, he will grow discouraged and may even want to reverse his decision. Yet, we human beings need to accept the stark reality that no easy improvisation of God's good-news story in our story will come this side of heaven! Then when discouragements come with our choices, we can face them with the knowledge that God's Spirit will continue to guide us in whatever fresh decisions we need to make in the midst of these struggles.

I have come to understand these matters through my own experience. Let me share a recent example. Two years ago a church in Australia offered me a wonderful ministry opportunity. Outwardly it presented many benefits and blessings for us as a family. I had about a month to decide. During this time I spoke about the possibility with people I trusted. I thought and prayed about whether to go or stay. I reflected on the feelings that my thoughts generated. Gradually the way ahead became clear to me. When I thought about leaving South Africa, I initially felt a sense of attraction about undertaking a new ministry in a new country. But as I stayed with this possibility, there emerged a strong undercurrent of unease and disquiet. The thought of leaving South Africa left me feeling out of sync with God's dream for my life.

In contrast, the option of remaining here in ministry left me with a strong, deep-down feeling of peace. Even though I felt unclear about what the future held for me, I had a persistent sense that South Africa was where I needed to continue improvising the missing act of God's good-news story in my life. So I decided to stay. While I take full responsibility for this decision, I also believe that the Holy Spirit guided me toward it. The consequences so far have been mixed. The year following the decision turned out to be a hard one. While some surprising options for creative and meaningful ministry opened, painful moments of disappointment and frustration also occurred. I affirmed yet again that there are pros and cons in every decision, even when we acknowledge the Holy Spirit's involvement in the decision-making process.

So we need to be clear about this. When decisions lead to difficult times, it does not mean the decisions were wrong. We do not need to reverse them. Know that even when we have made a poor choice and chosen the wrong road, God is not defeated nor will God abandon us on that road. God knows the desires of our hearts to be faithful. God will be with us, even on that wrong road, and can use us on that road if we seek to be obedient. We can continue to affirm that the Holy Spirit remains present in our experience. God is always bigger than the decisions we make, which enables us to place ourselves and our decisions in God's hands.

But we continue to reflect on our inner responses in order to be sensitive to how the Holy Spirit may be leading us forward. As we seek the Spirit's guidance for our lives, there seems to be, as one of my favorite Jesuit writers points out, a pattern of "reflection-action-reflection."[4] We reflect on a decision, act on it, and then reflect on that experience. That reflection leads to another decision and another action, followed by reflection. So the pattern continues. This insight can help us as we seek the Spirit's leading in whatever we may be going through right now as a result of past decisions.

Before I move on to the next section, I want to make one point quite clear. I do not want to limit the guidance of the Holy Spirit to the way described above. There are also times when the Holy Spirit "speaks" to us in other ways. Most often, this speaking takes the form of a certain kind of thought, a thought characterized by the quiet yet strong way it impresses itself on our mind. The content of the thought will also have a distinctive feel about it. It will never contradict the way of Christ or the witness of scripture. Indeed, this thought will often come to us while we read scripture and think about its meaning for our lives. However, I emphasize reflecting on the feelings that our thoughts generate as a way of listening to the Holy Spirit because it aids us in areas of decision making not specifically addressed by the scriptures.

GUIDES US IN CONSENSUS

One final thought. When it comes to learning about how the Holy Spirit guides us, you can read about an instructive moment in the life of the early church in Acts 15:1-29. To summarize simply, a big issue had arisen in Antioch. Some people in the church were teaching that in order to be made true believers newcomers had to be circumcised. After all, this is what the law of Moses taught. Paul and Barnabas disagreed fiercely with this view. These two, together with some elders from the local church community, traveled to meet with some Jerusalem leaders to discern God's way forward on this dispute about circumcision. The way this meeting unfolded teaches us a lot about the way the Holy Spirit uses consensus among Christ-followers to guide us.

First of all, we read how all the visitors from outside received a warm welcome, followed by a sharing of the exciting works that God had been doing in their midst. Then some believers in Jerusalem raised the circumcision issue. People at the meeting spoke on both sides of the issue—intensely, honestly, and respectfully. Finally, James from the Jerusalem community stood up and made a clear proposal with regard to the next step. A letter would be sent to the Antioch believers stating that Gentile believers were brothers and sisters in the same faith-family even though they had not been circumcised and that the men would not need to be circumcised. This letter contains a significant phrase that describes how the gathering in Jerusalem had come to this decision. It states, "It seemed good to the Holy Spirit and to us" (Acts 15:28).

These words suggest a process of prayerful conversation, with the conversational partners sharing their differing views on the matter at hand until all parties come together in consensus. This work of bringing people of various opinions to agreement is understood as the Holy Spirit's activity. No decision has been imposed or forced on people. Rather, persons share their differing thoughts and feelings in honest conversation. Openhearted listening and a confident trust in the Holy Spirit to bring about a common mind result in a creative solution. I wonder if you have ever experienced a similar happening in your life when facing a crucial situation.

SOME PERSONAL EXAMPLES

I have experienced the Holy Spirit's guidance through consensus in many situations. One of these has been in my marriage and family. When facing an important decision that affects our life together, I always share it with Debbie and ask for her thoughts and feelings. I do not believe that God will lead her in one direction and me in another direction. As a result, we have never made an important decision until both she and I have experienced an authentic sense of peace about what we decide to do. We have followed this method when choosing where to live, when deciding to make a significant purchase or not, when wondering how to respond to a crisis, and in many other domestic and vocational situations. Not only has this approach to decision making strengthened the bond between us, it has also given me greater confidence that the Holy Spirit leads our decision making.

I recall the time Debbie and I bought our first home. We had never owned property before but had saved up over the years. Then several years ago we decided to buy a house on our limited budget. We prayed, shared our hopes with God, and looked at one property after another. Sometimes I liked a house, and Debbie did not. Sometimes it was the other way round. One Saturday morning I had stayed home to watch some rugby while Debbie had gone to see a house for sale. She phoned me and said I needed to come round quickly. When I walked into the house for the first time, my heart leapt! She had experienced the same thing. We went home, talked together, looked at our available finances, and made our decision. We put in an offer to buy. I still have on my cell phone the message Debbie sent me the day after we had made this decision.

> Hi there, Trevor. I feel excited and right about our decision to buy the house. I think we can make it into a lovely home. It has been good to work together on this with you. Love you.
>
> —Debbie

I have also experienced the Holy Spirit's leading through consensus in the local congregation. When I pastored my first congregation, one of the leadership's primary decisions involved this principle. As a group of leaders we determined that we would make a decision only if there were consensus among us on the matter at hand. This decision rested on the conviction that the Holy Spirit would not lead us in different directions when it came to making decisions affecting our life as a church. Unity of heart and mind would matter more than majority rule. We agreed to follow this basic principle in all our decision making. While it sometimes slowed business down, when we made decisions we sensed that "the Holy Spirit and we had agreed" on the way forward. It was an exciting journey in being Spirit-led together.

I recall the congregation's decision to build a new sanctuary. When the idea was first raised, the leaders held divided feelings. We could easily have taken a vote and implemented majority rule. The pressure to follow this route was strong. But we decided to stick to the principle of consensus. We talked and listened to one another and prayed. Over time we all came to understand—even those of us initially opposed to building—that we needed to build. We shared the decision with our people. Their response was immediate. The vision captured their imagination. Even though we operated with limited financial resources, when we opened the doors of the sanctuary for the first time, we did not owe a cent to anyone.

The third place where I have experienced the Holy Spirit guiding me through consensus is in conversations with friends around God's call in my life. Personal calling is always moving and dynamic. It is seldom static and unchanging but rather unfolds gradually in the various seasons of our lives. As I try to live into the unfolding shape of God's calling in the sixth decade of my life, I have greatly valued talking with friends who give me honest feedback. I wrestle with many questions around God's personal call at the moment. Where can I best contribute to God's work? How can I best use my limited time and energy? Which ministry opportunities do I accept, and which do I turn down? How do I balance giving myself to others and enjoying myself with those closest to me? It is as I reflect on these questions with close companions that the Holy Spirit leads me forward most often. Usually, this leading comes with a consensus feeling around the decision that "this way feels right to the Holy Spirit and to us."

I chose to write this book out of this kind of consensus. I had already begun another book when I decided to write this one. The change in direction happened in this way. Whenever I thought about spending time writing the other book, I felt heavyhearted and sluggish. Then on the Monday after Pentecost Sunday, while driving home from an early morning appointment, I found myself thinking about writing a book on the Holy Spirit. Over the next few days I talked over the idea with some trusted friends. Their feedback and questions further clarified my thought of changing direction. Finally I put the writing of the other book on hold for the time being and began this one. While I take full responsibility for this decision, I am grateful to those with whom I was able to talk about it. I took their agreement and affirmation about the change of direction, together with what I was feeling and thinking in my heart and mind, as a leading from the Spirit to start writing this book.

DISCERNMENT

Each day presents us with countless choices. Some are significant. "Should I change jobs?" "Must I tell my kids about my diagnosis of cancer?" "Should I mention to my friend how his comments hurt me last night?" "How do I talk with my partner about my unhappiness in our relationship?" Some may seem rather trivial. "Shall we go to the movies tonight?" "What will I make for supper?" "What do I wear for the interview?" If we want to become more responsive to the Holy Spirit's leading, we need to discern the Spirit's movement in our lives. Discernment, as one of my favorite writers puts it, involves practice in prayerful attention to the inner movements of our hearts, prayerful reflection on them, and honest appraisal of what seems most in tune with God's purposes.[5]

This sounds like quite a mouthful, so let me take you through a simple exercise. First of all, invite God to be with you in this process. Tell God that you really want to follow and be obedient wherever the Holy Spirit may lead. This is an important part of the exercise. You are sharing with God your intention to be faithful no matter what God may want you to do. You need to be honest about this. If you are ambivalent about doing God's will, share these mixed feelings with God. You can pray something like, "God, there is one part of me that wants to do your will and another part of me that doesn't. Please help me to want to do your will with all of myself." God meets us where we are.

Next, think about the issue you are facing right now about which you need to make a decision. Do not evaluate its importance too quickly. Many everyday decisions have huge implications. Choices, as we know, always have consequences. I find it helpful to write down the issue that is facing me on a piece of paper, together with any thoughts that may come while thinking about it. Most probably, there will be a number of possible choices open to you regarding this particular matter. Again you may want to note these different choices. Continue to do all this as consciously as you can in God's presence, in an atmosphere of prayer, and with an openness to follow however the Spirit may lead you.

The third step may take a few hours. Imagine yourself making a certain choice. Stay with it as you go about your day. See yourself following this decision; then stop and evaluate how you feel in your heart about this decision. Are you at peace with it? Is it in sync with all that you know of God from your understanding of the scriptures? Does it seem to lead toward greater faith, hope, and love in your heart? Or does it, on the other hand, leave you with a sense of disquiet and unease? Repeat this process with each of the possible options. Keep yourself open to whatever path the Holy Spirit may lead. Record your thoughts if you can.

At this point, the discerning occurs. You pay attention to the feelings that your thoughts about the different options create in you. You are trying to discern which option brings you a deeper sense of peace. The Holy Spirit usually leads where there is a strong sense of God's peace. More often than not, feelings of joy and well-being will accompany this peace. The general rule of thumb underlying the approach is this: If our basic orientation in life is an honest desire to do God's will, it follows that whatever decision is in tune with God's purposes for our lives will bring us peace and joy. When a decision is not in sync with God's purposes, it will cause us to feel at odds with God and leave us unsettled and uneasy.

The final step in this discernment process involves actually making your decision and going ahead with it. If you consider it to be a weighty decision, it will be wise and helpful to talk over your decision with trusted friends before moving ahead. In other words, you do your best to discern God's way forward for your life, as well as pay attention to the thinking of those around you about the matter at hand. This is where the principle of consensus comes in. Faithful discernment in decision making is seldom an individual enterprise. More often than not, the Holy Spirit guides us through both our own thinking and the feelings it generates, as well as through the insights that come from others.

You may find the above process rather laborious. I have discovered that the more I practice it, the more it becomes part of the way I live. It is like learning to drive a four-speed car. At first, moving through the gears requires intense concentration and effort. Over time, changing gears becomes more natural, easy, and flowing. Something similar happens with the practice of discernment. As we go through the above steps of discerning God's way in our lives, it initially feels a bit mechanical. But as the Holy Spirit meets us in these efforts, the discerning process becomes easier and freer. We begin to see why discernment in the Bible is both something that comes from God and something that we have to do. (See 1 Cor. 12:10; 1 Thess. 5:21.)

When we have decisions to make, we need to hand ourselves over to the Holy Spirit. Rather than trying to guide the Holy Spirit, we allow the Holy Spirit to guide us. Too often we make our decisions and claim the Spirit's guidance afterward. Instead, as we improvise the missing act in God's good-news story in our story, we must listen to the promptings of the Holy Spirit. Thankfully, this listening is more possible than we think. The Holy Spirit is always present with us, always communicating within our experiences, in order to guide us in all our decision making. Let us resolve to give ourselves over in every way to the inner guidance of the Holy Spirit, who is truly our best spiritual director!

SMALL-GROUP CONVERSATION STARTERS

Icebreaker: What is your approach to making decisions?

1. How do you go about seeking God's will for your life?
2. How do you respond to the idea of improvising God's will in the way outlined in the chapter?
3. How do you discern the movements of the Holy Spirit in your life?
4. In what ways do you invite the help of others in your decision making?
5. Share one area of your present life where you are seeking to discern God's way for your life.

SIX

THE GIFT GOD GIVES

. . . Helps Us to Pray

One day little Johnny was spending time with his granny. She was sitting in front of the mirror, rubbing cream into her face, as many grannies do. The conversation went like this:

"Granny, what are you doing?"

"I am rubbing cream into my face."

"Why are you doing that Granny?"

"I want my wrinkles to go away."

Johnny became curious. He went closer, took a long look at his granny's face, and replied, "Granny, it's not working!"

Prayer sometimes feels like this. The reasons will vary. We wonder whether our prayers make any difference at all. We hear ourselves repeating the same words, or we do not know what words to use. We feel as if our prayers hit the ceiling and bounce back. God doesn't seem to do anything. We feel as if we are talking to ourselves. We think to ourselves, *Surely God cannot be in contact with all seven billion of us human beings at the same time.* The list is as long as the number of people who pray. Consider for a moment why you sometimes wonder whether prayer is worth the effort and the time.

Thankfully, even some biblical heroes struggled with prayer. Consider the apostle Paul, for example. We might not think that a leader of the early church would ever have struggled with prayer. Paul seems to be in a class above most of us ordinary people when it comes to matters of faith. His recorded prayers in the New Testament brim with confidence, boldness, and trust. Yet he describes himself as a fellow struggler when it comes to prayer. Look with me for a moment at chapter 8 of Paul's letter to the Romans.

Notice Paul's words about prayer that come halfway through the chapter. He writes unashamedly, "We do not know how to pray as we ought" (v. 26, NRSV). He does not tell his readers that *they* do not know how to pray. He does not set himself above others as one who knows everything about prayer. Rather, by using the plural pronoun "we," he identifies with all of us who sometimes have trouble with prayer. Paul's openness encourages our openness about our struggles with prayer.

One day, after I had finished preaching, I received a note requesting that I visit someone lying critically ill in a nearby hospital. When I got to the intensive care unit, the nurse showed me to the man's bed. No one else was with him. He appeared to be in a partial coma, hooked up to a respirator, struggling to breathe. As I leaned over his motionless body, I had no idea what or how to pray. I had experienced this inability to give words to prayer at other times. Often, whether it concerns praying for the healing of someone terminally ill or for larger issues like the people of Japan in the aftermath of the earthquake and tsunami, I find myself at a loss for words. I take comfort in knowing that Paul faced this issue too.

But Paul has some good news about the situation! Immediately after sharing his struggle with prayer, he goes on to say (in the remainder of that verse) that when we do not know how to pray or what to pray for, the "Spirit intercedes with sighs too deep for words" (NRSV). Paul has discovered a truth about prayer that we must never forget. We are not on our own when it comes to our praying. The Holy Spirit's active presence connects us to the living God in a vital way. For this reason, we can boldly affirm that *the Holy Spirit helps us in our praying.*

Let us explore Paul's development of this affirmation in the eighth chapter of Romans. I have often told my family members that if they are with me while I am dying, this is the chapter I would like them to read to me over and over again. For me, this passage puts words to the profound mystery of what it means to live with God in the midst of our suffering world. Most especially, we find in this chapter valuable clues about how the Spirit helps us to pray when we do not know how to pray or what to pray for. I hope that exploring these clues will deepen your prayer relationship with God as it has mine over the years.

THE ABBA EXPERIENCE

The Holy Spirit helps us in our praying by enabling us to call God "Abba." It is one thing to acknowledge God formally in our prayers as our heavenly parent. It is completely another matter for us to know God intimately as our Abba when we pray. We yearn for the latter experience, especially when we battle with praying. We want to know that we are not orphans in this universe. We want to know when we pray that we belong to God in a deep, personal, and unshakable way, whatever we may be going through. Paul tells us what the Holy Spirit does for us: We receive the Holy Spirit and we cry out, "*Abba,* Father" (Rom. 8:15).

Abba is the word Jesus used when he spoke with God. Where did he get it? Growing up in a devout Jewish family, he would have been familiar with all the well-known Old Testament titles for God: Lord, King, Rock, Redeemer, Mighty One, Shepherd, Deliverer; yes, and also Father in a more formal sense. But when he prays he does not use any of these words. He calls God, *Abba*, the Aramaic word that Jesus would have used as a child when he addressed his father, Joseph. When Jesus addressed God in this way, it would have surprised those around him. This was not the usual Jewish term of address for God. The term evokes images of a tender intimacy between Jesus and his heavenly Father.

We need to go one step further. Not only did Jesus express a familial relationship with God, he wanted his followers to do the same. You may remember the moment when he made this clear. Luke's Gospel recounts a time when Jesus was praying. As he finished, his disciples, perhaps feeling the same kind of inadequacy about their praying that Paul would express later in his letter to the Romans, ask him to teach them how to pray. When Jesus responds, he tells them to begin their prayer by addressing God in the same way that he did. When you pray, Jesus tells them, say "Father." They must have been astonished! Jesus was opening up a whole new way of praying for them that had not been possible before he came. They now can express their relationship to God using Jesus' more familial term of address.

And so can you and I! According to Paul, we too can experience the astonishing reality of speaking to God as our *Abba* when we pray. It is not an experience that we achieve, manufacture, or earn. Nor does it depend on any special skill, talent, or ability. The only thing that matters is our openness to the Spirit who works in our hearts and who helps us to cry out to God, "*Abba*, Father!" Even when we do not know how to pray or what to pray for, we can know God in this tender and intimate way. Through the Holy Spirit, Jesus wants to share his own experience of God as *Abba*. This inner assurance is one way the Holy Spirit helps in our praying.

HEALING NEGATIVE FATHERHOOD IMAGES

Now, I acknowledge that this image of God as Father may be disturbing and painful for some reading this book. Perhaps this is true for you. It could be that the word *Father* triggers in your heart and mind images of violence, abuse, betrayal, marital unfaithfulness, drunkenness, or some other destructive experience. Maybe you do not remember your father or know who he is. Before I suggest a possible way forward, I want to say that, even as I write these words, I pray for you. May you come to know in your own experience the grace and healing that constantly flows from the heart of Jesus' *Abba* into our broken world. God's touching our lives and the wounds of our childhood can bring great blessing.

What can help us if we struggle with the image of God as Father? Let me share a few thoughts. First, it may help to remember that God is much more than a father in a human sense. God is the Creator, not a procreator. As the *Abba* of Jesus, God is not simply male or female. We dare not load onto God only male characteristics. The Bible constantly stresses both the fatherly and motherly qualities of God. Therefore, as Albert Nolan points out, the significance of Jesus' use of the term *Abba* is not that it is masculine or even that it is a word a child might use, but that it expresses intimacy. Like the love of a good parent, God's love for us is always warm, tender, and unconditional.[1]

If we have a negative father image, we might be able to recognize someone else in our personal history who has loved us well. Instead of our father, it may be our mother, a grandparent, a relative, a teacher, a friend, a counselor, or a pastor—someone who cared for us through thick and thin or hung in with us when we were going through a difficult time or patiently listened to us when we needed to speak or forgave us after we had messed up badly or affirmed and helped us to believe in ourselves when we faced a challenging situation. Most of us have had someone like this who has touched our lives at least once in our lifetime. Remembering such a person and feeling again the love that we received from him or her offers insight into God's intimate love for us.

We also can bring our painful memories of abuse by our fathers to God for healing. Usually this approach involves sharing our feelings of rejection and deprivation with a trusted spiritual friend or counselor. This person would be someone who can listen to us and pray with us. In my own ongoing experience of healing, I have discovered that when we do this, God can "re-parent" us. We begin to receive from God the unconditional acceptance and strong affirmation that we did not receive from our human fathers. We discover that we do not need to remain stuck in our painful past or in compensatory ways of behavior for what we lacked in our father-son/daughter relationship. We can experience a second "childhood" in which we grow up surrounded by God's unconditional, enfolding, and intimate love for us. Perhaps this is another aspect of what it means to be born again by the power of the Spirit.

GOD'S BELOVED CHILDREN

The Holy Spirit helps us in our praying by assuring us that we are God's beloved children. This follows on from knowing God as our Abba. If God is our heavenly parent, then we are God's sons and daughters. We are part of the family that God is forming to bless and to heal the world. When we open our lives to Christ, his Spirit goes deep into our hearts and tells us who we really are. The Holy Spirit assures us that God loves us with a relentless love that will never let us go and from which nothing can ever separate us. Paul states it beautifully: "The Spirit himself testifies with our spirit that we are God's children" (Rom. 8:16).

As a pastor for over thirty-five years, I have discovered how many people wrestle with understanding themselves as God's children. We may acknowledge the concept in our heads but not allow it to become a reality in our hearts. Many of us who have followed

Christ for years struggle with this notion. We know theoretically that God loves us, but we do not feel God's love deep down. Rather than experiencing ourselves as God's beloved children, we see ourselves a little on the outside of God's love. The journey from head to heart is often one of the longest we ever go on. But when it happens, it makes all the difference in how we pray.

Remember the prodigal son's homecoming from the distant country? (See Luke 15:11-32.) He had his speech ready. "Father, I have sinned against heaven and against you. I am no longer worthy to be called your son; make me like one of your hired servants." In effect, he was saying to his father, "After the terrible mess that I have made of my life, I can never hope to be your son again. I can never hope to relax with you in the lounge or eat with you in the kitchen or be part of the family circle again. Just give me a little room outside the house and treat me as one of your servants. That is all I deserve from you. I have lost my right to be your beloved child. I simply ask that you tolerate me."

I wonder if this is how you sometimes feel in your relationship with God. As a good friend of mine puts it, when we mess up like the prodigal son, it is as if the devil takes an aerosol can and sprays graffiti over the inner walls of our soul condemning us: *I know too much about you. I know what your heart is like. You can't bluff me. You are not worthy to be loved, accepted, and forgiven. Do not ever think that you can be God's child again or share in God's family. Just make sure that you behave yourself from now on if you want to be accepted. Maybe in the distant future, if you really deserve it, you might one day be acceptable to God again.* Can you identify with these thoughts? If these are your feelings in relationship with God, you will find it hard to relate to God in prayer.

Return to the story of the prodigal son once more. When he gets in sight of home, his father comes running down the road to meet him and flings his arms around him. The boy cannot even finish his carefully prepared speech. Before he gets to the part about being treated as a hired servant, the father interrupts him and says to the servants, "Quick! Bring the best robe and put it on him. Put a ring on his finger and sandals on his feet. Bring the fattened calf and kill it. Let's have a feast and celebrate. For this son of mine was dead and is alive again; he was lost and is found" (Luke 15:22-24). What these words must have meant to the boy! They would have convinced him that he was taken directly back into his father's joyful heart. He was the father's beloved child just as he was.

RECEIVING ASSURANCE OF OUR BELOVEDNESS

The Holy Spirit helps us confirm the assurance of our belovedness. If we listen carefully we will hear the Spirit saying to us in our depths, "You are Abba's beloved. You are loved, accepted, and forgiven. You belong to the family of God. You have complete access into God's presence. You don't have to send anyone else with your requests. You do not have to pretend to be what you are not. You can come as you are because you are relating to someone who loves you very much." Is this your experience in prayer, especially in those moments when you find it hard to know how or what to pray?

Our knowing ourselves as God's beloved allows us to pray simply, honestly, and directly. We do not need to role play before God. We do not need the right prayer-formula. We do not need to use fancy or big words. We do not need to have our motives correctly sorted out. We can come to God as our Abba and speak heart to heart with God. We share our pain, our disappointments, our joys, our temptations, our worries and ask God to supply our need. And if we do not know how to pray or don't even want to pray, we can be honest about this with God as well. By assuring us that we can come to God in this childlike way, the Spirit helps us along our journey of prayer.

Let me ask some personal questions: How do you see yourself in relation to God? Do you have the assurance that comes from knowing that you are God's son or daughter? How would you describe your sense of access into the heart of God that Jesus Christ makes possible? What words would you use to express your present experience of God's family? What would it be like for you to relate to God just as confidently as a child relates to a loving parent?

As you reflect on these questions I trust that you will come to know more deeply that you are Abba's child. When you do, you will move into an intimate and personal way of praying.

WE ARE ALWAYS PRAYED IN

The Holy Spirit helps us in our praying by praying within us. Here are Paul's intriguing words. Read them slowly and carefully.

> We do not know what we ought to pray for, but the Spirit himself intercedes for us through wordless groans. And he who searches our hearts knows the mind of the Spirit, because the Spirit intercedes for God's people in accordance with the will of God (Rom. 8:26-27).

There is a deep mystery here that we need to explore. Let me relate two thoughts about these verses that I find helpful. They have come to me through the writings of other Christ-followers who have encouraged me to enter into the experience described here by the apostle. I hope they will help you too.

On the one hand, Paul reminds us that a prayer meeting is going on within our lives 24/7. Think about this startling truth with me. Our hearts are constantly at prayer. Even when we don't believe we are praying, "someone" is praying deep within us. When we allow Christ to make his home within our lives, his Spirit brings to us the intensified gift of prayer. From the moment of conversion onward, we have a unique connection with God in our innermost depths, whether we feel it or not. All the time, but especially when we have no idea about how to pray, the Holy Spirit is praying inside you and me. And God knows and hears these prayers because they are always in tune with God's purposes for our lives and the life of our world. We are never without prayer!

This ongoing prayer of the Spirit does not mean that we can sit back and do nothing. Our responsibility comes in listening to the Spirit with a willingness to let the Spirit reshape the content of our prayers. As we do this, we will find our hearts gradually beginning to resonate more deeply with God's heartbeat for the healing of this world. We see this happening in Jesus' prayer in Gethsemane as he wrestled with his Father about the final step of his mission. (See Mark 14:32-36.) He began by praying that the cup be taken from him. "*Abba,* Father, everything is possible for you. Take this cup from me." But as he prayed, I believe the Spirit of Abba reshaped his prayer. The next line was, "Yet not what I will, but what you will." Now he was ready to go where Abba wanted him to go and to drink what Abba wanted him to drink. Can you see what it means to listen to the prayer that the Holy Spirit is praying within us and to realign our prayers with it?

So when we pray, we often begin by praying for whatever seems good to us, for whatever is on our hearts; but we listen carefully to the way the Spirit is praying within us. We do not need to be too mystical about this! We are not clueless about what the Spirit may be saying. As the Spirit of Jesus, the Holy Spirit takes the prayer of Jesus and prays it in our own depths. It is a prayer for God's kingdom to come, a prayer for God's name to be treasured, a prayer for God's will to be done, a prayer for heaven to come to earth, a prayer for the mending of our broken relationships and our broken world. Above all, it is a prayer for you and me to become the answers to our prayers in our daily lives, right where we are.

WITH GROANS THAT WORDS CANNOT EXPRESS

On the other hand, Paul teaches us that the Spirit prays within us with groans that words cannot express. The word *groans* suggests that the Holy Spirit prays deep within our souls, in those hidden places of our hearts where we wrestle to find the words for our feeling and thinking. You surely know what it is like to experience a powerful event in your life—perhaps a sigh of longing or an upsurge of praise or a cry of frustration—yet you battle to express it in the words that you have at your disposal. In moments like these, the Spirit draws out of us an inner groaning that goes far beyond ordinary speech that we recognize and understand. But thankfully the groaning is recognized and understood by the God who searches our hearts and who knows the mind of the Spirit.

I remember my first experience of this happening in my life. I was at university studying for pastoral ministry, a time of intellectual searching around the big questions of faith and belief. The pain of my country at that stage of its apartheid history weighed heavily on my heart. I found myself wrestling with what it meant to be a faithful follower of Jesus. One weekend I came home to stay with my parents. It was late at night, and I could not sleep. I got out of bed and knelt before God with all the tossings and turnings of my burdened heart struggling for expression. I could not find words to express what I was experiencing. As I began to speak to God, I heard unintelligible sounds coming from my mouth. Now I can only describe it as the groaning of my spirit calling out to God from my very depths—a sense of inner surrender and release.

The experience puzzled me for some time. Fortunately I had a good friend with whom I could speak about such matters. I asked him a number of questions. Was I making all this up? Was I deluding myself? Was it a sign of hysteria? Must I let it happen again? Was this what some called "praying in tongues"? My friend listened patiently and then asked one question: Had my experience drawn me closer to Jesus Christ or pushed me farther away from him?

Immediately I knew the answer. Against the background of my theological studies, with their heavy emphasis on the intellect, this experience had strengthened my heart-connection with God. When I replied in this way, he urged me always to be open to this experience in my life.

It turned out to be wise counsel. Throughout my journey with God I often have found it helpful to pray with groans that words cannot express. This approach has become a childlike and natural part of my relationship with God. Usually it results in a warming of my heart toward Christ. Sometimes it helps me share with God those things that I struggle to put into ordinary words. I encourage you to be open to whatever way the Spirit leads you. Many people do not experience this praying within in the same way others do. Certainly we never view this as a superior sign of the Holy Spirit's presence in someone's life. It is only one way the Spirit helps us pray when we don't know how.

One of my favorite stories about prayer seems quite relevant to this part of the chapter. A certain monk was a man of prayer to an extraordinary degree, someone who lived prayer every day of his life. One day a person asked him how he had reached this state. He replied that he found it hard to explain. "Looking back," he said, "my impression is that for many years I was carrying prayer within my heart but did not know it. It was like a spring, but one covered by a stone. Then at a particular moment Jesus took the stone away. At that, the spring began to flow and it has been flowing ever since."[3] Maybe we can ask Jesus to remove the stone from our hearts, so that the prayer that lies there like a hidden stream may begin to flow through our lives into our relationships and into God's world.

AFFIRMATIVE PRAYER

In exploring how the Holy Spirit helps us to pray, I have emphasized some powerful insights that Paul offers regarding our relationship with God. In Romans 8 he notes that as we follow Christ, the Holy Spirit helps us experience three truths: God is our Abba. We are God's beloved. We are always prayed in. These truths need to become part of who we are every waking moment. Whatever we are going through, and especially when we do not know how to pray, we acknowledge these truths in our hearts and minds. So we ask the Holy Spirit to help us partake more fully of these aspects of relationship with God. But we can build these truths into our lives by experimenting with the practice of affirmative prayer, or prayers of affirmation.

Let me describe what I mean by affirmative prayer. Prayers of affirmation focus on who we are in Christ. They take these identity-truths, murmur them with gratitude to God, and store them away in our hearts. In this chapter I have emphasized three such truths. There are many more, and they are well worth memorizing.[4] When we pray affirmatively, we are not petitioning God. Rather we are celebrating who we are and to whom we belong. We are not asking; we are affirming. We are not pleading; we are asserting. As we do this, we could say that in affirmative prayer we stack the mental firewood that the Holy Spirit can one day fan into a blazing fire.

I find affirmative prayer most beneficial before I get out of bed. When I first open my eyes in the morning I often feel overwhelmed by some dark and difficult emotions. Sometimes I feel despondent; at other times I sense an anxious knot in my stomach. Then there are those times when I just want to pull the covers over my head and go back to sleep. In moments like this I usually pray affirmatively, taking some of the truths of my identity in Christ and going over them a few times before I get up. A good place to start, I want to suggest, is by praying affirmatively the three insights about our identity in Christ that we explored in this chapter.

First of all, with regard to God's being our Abba, accept Jesus' offer of this intimate relationship with God and thank him for it. Begin whispering to God over and over again, "*Abba.*" Let the sense of security, tenderness, care, and love that this word for God often brings flow through you. Bask in the experience. Allow the good memories of your childhood relationships with your mother and father, and the warm feelings associated with them, to nourish your Abba-experience. If you have painful memories of your parents, call to mind someone who touched your life with love. Let these memories lead you into the infinitely deeper love that Abba has for you every moment of your life.

Next, add to this affirmation the powerful truth of your being God's beloved child. Consider repeating the phrase, "Abba, I belong to you." Use your breathing as an aid to prayer. As you inhale, you may want to say "Abba," and as you exhale, "'I belong to you." Be mindful as you pray affirmatively that this method lies beyond fuzzy sentimentality or wishful thinking. You affirm powerful truths about who you are as a follower of Christ and plant them within your heart and mind. From here they will affect the emotional and mental tones of your life more than you know. Indeed, I have sometimes found these words resonating within me during the day, even when I have not consciously chosen to repeat them.

One more truth to build into your affirmative prayer is this: The Holy Spirit prays within you. You can turn this truth into an affirmation by adding another line to the above phrase: "Abba, I belong to you. Your Spirit prays within me." Praying these sentences affirmatively will lead you to wonder how the Holy Spirit may be praying within you. In all likelihood the Spirit will be taking the prayer of Jesus for heaven to come to earth and applying it specifically to your personal circumstances, life, and world. Often, when I affirm these truths, I receive promptings about a person I need to call or of some good that I can do for another or of a broken aspect of my life that requires attention. I am learning to take these promptings seriously and have been amazed by the outcome.

A word of caution is in order as we experiment with prayers of affirmation. With affirmative prayer we are not trying to force ourselves to believe something that is not true. For example, to offer a person with rheumatoid arthritis the following affirmation: "Because God is in me, I can move around freely," is both cruel and blasphemous. Affirmative prayer speaks the truth of who we are and to whom we belong *in Christ*. It is a down-to-earth way to place different aspects of our identity before God and plant them in the deeper levels of our beings. We can employ this type of prayer before getting out of bed, when going to bed, in fixed times of prayer, or in those odd moments of our days when we are not thinking about anything in particular.

I hope that you will experiment with affirmative prayer. Be patient with yourself. This method of praying is not acquired overnight. However if you persevere, especially in those moments when you struggle to pray, it could open you to the Holy Spirit's assistance. Whatever may happen in or around you, you can boldly affirm these truths: "God is my Abba. I am God's beloved. I am prayed in." All the time!

SMALL-GROUP CONVERSATION STARTERS

Icebreaker: Share one of your earliest memories of praying.

1. Describe your life of prayer at the moment.
2. In what area do you struggle most when it comes to prayer?
3. How meaningful to you is the image of God as "*Abba,* Father"?
4. With whom do you identify most in the parable of the prodigal son?
5. How would your praying change if you believed that the Holy Spirit is praying within you all the time?

SEVEN

THE GIFT GOD GIVES

. . . Empowers Us to Be Witnesses

Two men traveled to work together each day. From Monday to Friday they worked as colleagues in the same company. Over weekends they would go their separate ways. On Sundays the one would play golf, the other would go to church. One Monday as they drove to work, the golfer fired an unexpected question at his churchgoing friend: "When are you going to stop this hypocrisy of going to church each week?"

"What do you mean?" responded the churchgoer defensively. "I am not a hypocrite. Sunday worship is very important to me."

"Well, if you believe that to be true, then I am missing out on a great deal," said the golfer, "yet you have never shared with me what Jesus means to you."

I refuse to throw stones at the man who felt hesitant about sharing his faith. Perhaps he had good reasons for being a reluctant witness. Maybe he did not want to come across as pushy or arrogant or disrespectful. Nevertheless, I find this true story challenging. It gets me thinking about how many people could confront me in a similar way. I feel sure that a number of people could say to me, "Trevor, I have known you for many years. Almost every Sunday you go to church. Yet not once have you shared with me what Jesus means to you."

THE CHALLENGE OF WITNESSING

Witnessing about Jesus Christ requires prayerful thought. Christ-followers sometimes relay their faith in a way that betrays the gospel itself. Think of the large-scale tragedies like the Crusades, the Inquisition, and even those well-intentioned missionary efforts that have trampled over local traditions and customs. On a personal level we may tell others about our faith in ways that are neurotic, toxic, and ideological. I often cringe when I remember some of my efforts at faith sharing. One embarrassing memory from early in my faith journey always springs to mind.

It usually occurred on Sunday afternoons. I would stand at the side of the main road in Port Elizabeth with my friend Philip, thumbing a lift from the passing traffic. We had no specific destination in mind. All we wanted to do was to get into the car of an unsuspecting motorist so that we could pass on the good news. As you can imagine, once we were inside, the driver had no option but to listen to us. When we had said our piece, we asked to be dropped off. We would then walk across the road and repeat the process with another motorist heading back to where we had come from!

My recollection of my early witnessing efforts brings mixed feelings. On one hand, I do not feel good about how I went about sharing my newfound faith. I wonder how many people I may have put off the Christian faith for life! On the other hand, I am also aware that from the early stages of my faith journey, I have desired to tell others about Christ. This yearning has grown stronger in recent years. The question, however, is this: How do we witness in a way that remains faithful to the gospel, rings true with our lives, and is helpful to others?

At this point we desperately need the Holy Spirit's strength and guidance. Before his ascension, Jesus instructed his followers not to leave Jerusalem until they received the promised gift of the Holy Spirit. They were not to try to go it alone or think that it all depended on them. Rather they were to be empowered by God's Spirit before they went out as witnesses to the Messiah.

One author has pointed out that we need to explore what the Holy Spirit adds to our natural human capacities, without which we cannot even begin to be witnesses for Christ.[1] How does this power help us bear witness to the gospel of Jesus Christ? These are critical explorations and deserve our thoughtful reflection. Here are some of my thoughts.

POWER TO KNOW CHRIST PERSONALLY

First of all, the Holy Spirit empowers us to know Jesus Christ personally. Reliable witnesses always know something firsthand. They do not just believe something or feel something or hope something. The other night my son, Mark, and I witnessed a horrific hit-and-run accident. It happened right in front of us as we waited at a traffic light. When the police later asked Mark to make a statement about the accident, Mark could relay what he personally had seen. If he had been able to tell the police only what he believed or felt or hoped, he would have been of little use as a witness. His effective witness hinged on his ability to describe his experience.

Similarly, our task as followers of Christ is to know him firsthand and, in knowing him in this way, to be able to make him known to others. This firsthand knowledge is essential if we are to be reliable witnesses. This is as true for our relationship with Christ as it is for our relationships with one another.

Through the Holy Spirit, we come to know Jesus Christ personally. Rather than giving us new theoretical knowledge about Christ, the Holy Spirit takes what we have read and heard about Jesus and makes these things real for us. Doctrines about Jesus Christ are important, but we need to experience that he is alive and at work in our world today if we are going to be his witnesses. The Holy Spirit makes this firsthand knowledge of Christ possible for you and me. Jesus himself explained that the Holy Spirit would do this for us: "He will glorify me because it is from me that he will receive what he will make known to you" (John 16:14).

The Bible tells us that we are loved, accepted, and forgiven by God in Jesus Christ. The Holy Spirit makes this real for us. The Bible tells us that Jesus Christ died for our sins. The Holy Spirit makes this real for us. The Bible tells us that Jesus Christ has risen from the dead, defeated the dark powers, and lives beyond crucifixion. The Holy Spirit makes this real for us. The Bible tells us that Jesus Christ is the promised Messiah and Lord of the whole world. The Holy Spirit makes this real for us. The Holy Spirit leads us to know that we are called to witness that Jesus Christ is indeed the risen and ascended Lord.

A PERSONAL TESTIMONY

Perhaps I shall relate a little of my personal testimony in this regard. As I explained earlier in this book, I was a searching teenager when Jesus Christ first made himself known to me. The first big truth I learned about Jesus was that he loves me, died

for me, rose again, and is alive today. I enjoyed singing the chorus
(and still do!):

> *He is Lord, he is Lord!*
> *He is risen from the dead and he is Lord!*
> *Every knee shall bow, every tongue confess*
> *that Jesus Christ is Lord.*

These words seemed to bring together all my discoveries about Jesus.
They also put their finger on why I wanted to follow him as his
disciple for the rest of my life.

However, there is this huge difference between *knowing about*
and *knowing through* direct acquaintance. I needed to get to know
the living Lord in my own life. I needed to experience the power
of his loving presence in my wrestling with temptation, in my weak-
nesses and struggles, in my speaking and behavior, in my relationships and work. As I have consciously sought to keep my life open
to the work of the Holy Spirit over the years, I can say that this
process has taken place gradually. While I desire an experience of
much more of Christ's love, I am grateful for what the Holy Spirit
has already revealed in my heart.

Let me tell you one way the Holy Spirit has helped me to know
Christ more personally. Persons close to me know that I have struggled over the years with my sense of worth and value. For reasons
that go deeper than the conscious, I have found it hard to acknowledge in my heart that I am God's beloved. My inability has often
resulted in destructive behavior patterns that have left me battered
in spirit, weary in body, and estranged in my closest relationships.
Even though I knew intellectually that God loved me, my heart did
not seem to grasp this amazing reality. There seemed to be a wide
gap between my head and my heart.

Today I thank God that the gap has slowly been bridged. Even
though I continue to wrestle with intellectual doubts and faith-
questions, I have received an ever-deepening assurance about some

matters. I now know that I am Abba's beloved. I know that I am a special person loved by Christ. I know that I belong in God's family. I know that nothing can separate me from the love of God in Jesus Christ. Over time the Holy Spirit has taken what I knew with my head and placed it in my heart. Today this personal heart-knowledge forms the foundation of my witness to Jesus Christ.

POWER TO COMMUNICATE CHRIST

Second, the Holy Spirit gives us the power necessary to communicate Christ so that others can come to know him. Read about the first Christian Pentecost in Acts 2. Jesus' followers were gathered together when the Holy Spirit came among them. Luke uses the images of "the blowing of a violent wind" and "tongues of fire" to describe the terrifying and exhilarating activity of the Holy Spirit in their midst. Small wonder that a handful of disciples without formal position or title soon became a force to be reckoned with throughout the ancient world.

The first coming of the Holy Spirit brought the miracle of communication. When the disciples began to speak and preach about the amazing things that God had done in Jesus Christ, everyone in that cosmopolitan crowd heard them speaking in their own language. They did not need a translator to understand. It was a miracle accomplished by the Holy Spirit. This aspect may surprise us. Usually we associate speaking in tongues with unintelligible sounds and syllables. This Pentecostal experience of tongues differed.

Over the years I have listened to people describe this kind of experience. Usually what happens is that someone, prompted by the Holy Spirit, speaks in a language he or she doesn't recognize— only to discover that someone in the group recognizes the language and understands what is being said. I have no reason to doubt those who describe such experiences. Certainly these well-attested reports remind us that God can do whatever God desires and that we need to avoid bounding how the Holy Spirit empowers us to communicate the gospel to those around us.

But, you may ask, what does this Pentecostal experience mean for those of us who want to be witnesses for Christ in the more ordinary situations we find ourselves in each day? Simply this: It reminds us that witnessing involves more than verbal transmission of information about Christ from one person to another. Instead it involves our participation in a miracle of communication between people in which the Holy Spirit makes known the reality of Jesus Christ to the people we are with. That reflects the disciples' experience with the crowd in Jerusalem. Without being caught up in the current of the Holy Spirit, the disciples would have been unable to communicate Christ to the crowd around them. And neither would we!

LISTENING AND SPEAKING

When we consider sharing Christ with those around us, we need to remind ourselves of our total dependence on the Holy Spirit. The Holy Spirit is already at work in the lives of those around us before we arrive. The Holy Spirit continuously reaches out to people through their experiences of human love, wonder, and longing from the beginning of their lives. Even in experiences of pain and struggle, they are being touched by the Holy Spirit who seeks to bring comfort. Often our first task in witnessing is simply to come alongside the other person and to help him or her recognize God's Spirit already at work in their life.

For this reason, we remind ourselves again that witnessing about Christ will always involve listening. We listen to other persons' questions, longings, and struggles. We listen to how they describe their life situations. We listen to their joys and sorrows. We listen to their objections to the Christian faith and to the Christian church. One of our greatest mistakes is to focus on the telling part without an equal emphasis on the listening part. We assume that we know what they need without first listening to them, a deeply arrogant assumption that short-circuits a meaningful connection.

I once came across a cartoon that depicted two gangs attacking each other. One gang was people from the church carrying a banner that read, "Christ is the answer." The other gang, obviously not from the church, carried a banner that read, "What is the question?" This cartoon challenges us to get the balance right between listening and talking when it comes to witnessing for Christ. We need not only the Holy Spirit's gift of tongues; we also need the Holy Spirit to give us the gift of ears! When we open our ears in conscious listening, the Holy Spirit draws us into the Pentecostal miracle of communication through which Christ makes known his loving presence.

But the moment comes when we use words to share what we know of Christ. We do this honestly, depending on the Holy Spirit. I don't know about you, but I really want to be able to speak about my experience of Christ in a way that touches other people. To use the language of Acts, I long to speak in the "tongues" of the young and the elderly, the rich and the poor, the learned and the simple, so that just like the Pentecost crowd each will hear about the love of God revealed in Jesus Christ in his or her own language. Before every conversation with a spiritual seeker or struggler, I will inwardly pray, "Lord, may your Spirit give me the words that this human heart needs to hear."

But what do I say? you may wonder. No set formula or three-point presentation or illustration exists. The Holy Spirit will supply the words if you ask. God's Spirit will help you put into credible words what you have come to know about Christ; the ways in which you have experienced Christ in your times of failure, struggle, and weakness. In the moments when you share your faith, those listening to you do not need to know what a great person you are. Spirit-prompted witnessing will move them to think more about the wisdom, the power, and the amazing grace of Jesus Christ. For this is what the Holy Spirit always communicates.

POWER TO LAY DOWN OUR LIVES

Third, the Holy Spirit empowers us to lay down our lives like Jesus did. This may sound rather melodramatic, but let me explain. The Greek word for martyr (marturos) simply means "witness." A martyr in the first-century world of the Bible was a person who could give credible witness. You may then wonder why today we call people who suffer and die for their faith martyrs. In preparing to give themselves in this costly way for their faith, these martyrs bore witness to a truth so evident for them that it was worth suffering and dying for. If we are going to sacrifice ourselves for the sake of the gospel, we will need the power of the Holy Spirit more than we realize.

The first disciple recorded as a witness-martyr in the early church was Stephen. Let me briefly sketch his story: He was a deacon. Very quickly he found himself embroiled in conflict with the Jewish religious leadership. His preaching about Jesus threatened the Jewish belief system. He was brought before the religious legal body known as the Sanhedrin where he was asked to defend himself against a charge of blasphemy. In an astonishing and masterful speech he continued to witness boldly to the gospel of Jesus Christ. As a result, he received the death penalty of stoning.

Many religious martyrs throughout history have died as they violently sought to take the lives of those they opposed; others have been killed calling down judgment and curses on their killers. Stephen's death differed radically. As his body was broken and he was crushed to death by the rocks hurled by his accusers, he prayed that God would not hold their sin against them. Only one explanation for this Christlike response of nonretaliation and forgiveness exists. The Holy Spirit who had dwelt in Jesus Christ had now filled Stephen and given him the strength to suffer and die.

This form of costly and sacrificial witness to Jesus Christ continues into the present day. The twentieth century saw more martyrs than any previous century. We can only wonder what will happen in this century. I hope that you and I will not be called to be martyrs with outward wounds and scars or even perhaps to give our life. But we will be called to bear those scars and wounds that come from loving people deeply. In this way we can bear credible witness to a scarred and wounded living Christ. But if we are going to lay down our lives in the way Jesus did, or like Stephen did, then like them we can be sure that we will need the strength and power of the Holy Spirit to remain faithful.

WHAT SACRIFICE MAY MEAN FOR US

Let me be more specific. Try to think for a moment how we need the Holy Spirit to empower us if we are going to lay down our lives in our closest relationships. We will certainly struggle in the strength of our own willpower to make sacrifices joyfully for those we love, to listen attentively to our partner when we are tired, to stay connected when we feel hurt or let down, to reach out when all we want to do is withdraw into our needs, and so on. We can do these kinds of things with joy and delight and self-abandonment only when we have help from beyond ourselves. Try to behave in the above fashion by relying on your own strength over a period of time and see what happens. We need the Spirit's power.

I recall my mother's care for my father when he suffered from Alzheimer's disease. Every day for almost two years she would get a ride to the assisted-living complex where Dad spent his last days. Day after day she would sit with him, sometimes in the silence, thumb through picture books with him, help him cut up his food for lunch, play his favorite music, take him for a walk around the block, try to understand his confused speech. In these ways, my mother laid down her life for my dad. When asked how she did it, she would always reply, "With help from above."

Think too of our need of the Holy Spirit's strength if we are to lay down our lives for our suffering neighbors. We cannot do this if we depend only on our own human strength. We will burn out, become totally overwhelmed, or give up. We need the inexhaustible resources of God's Spirit to enter the pain of others and to walk with them in their troubles. We learn this from those who have given themselves to those who suffer. Whether it is a Mother Teresa or our own mothers, those who have laid down their lives for others have been able to do so because of the Holy Spirit's empowerment.

We will definitely need the Holy Spirit to empower us if we are going to lay down our lives to create a more just and compassionate society, modeled on the heart of Christ. Whether this means refusing to be part of an evil practice or blowing the whistle on corruption or confronting someone about his or her abusive behavior or challenging our local congregation to be more inclusive of those who differ in color or class or sexual orientation, we will need the power of the Holy Spirit. Otherwise we struggle to approach these actions in a Christlike way.

Today so many words come at us from all directions telling us about Jesus. Tragically, they sometimes sound glib. Sometimes they simply do not ring true and echo with hollowness. But sometimes the words powerfully connect. They pierce our hearts and go to the root of our being. They sound honest, real, and believable. They affect our lives in a radically different manner. As I reflect on what makes the difference in impact, I have come to believe that it is all about the life of the person speaking. When the life of the person speaking is a living, breathing example of the laid-down life of Jesus, the Holy Spirit speaks powerfully. When the life of the person speaking contradicts the laid-down life of Jesus, the Holy Spirit seems strangely silent.

Let me summarize the main ideas of this chapter. We are called to be witnesses to Jesus Christ. This witnessing occurs through our listening, our lips, and our lives. To witness effectively about the reality of the living Christ, we need his Spirit to empower us. The Holy Spirit does this by empowering us to know Christ personally, to communicate Christ to those around us, and to lay down our lives like Jesus did. The Holy Spirit adds this kind of strength to our natural capacities and abilities. The crucial question is this: Will we allow the Holy Spirit to empower us to become credible witnesses for Jesus Christ?

PRAYERFUL WATCHING AND WAITING

Timing is integral when it comes to witnessing about God's good-news story. When we speak at the wrong time, our words about Jesus Christ are often resented by those who need to hear. They may be interpreted as pushy, self-righteous, or judgmental. So we practice how to pray, watch, and wait—to watch the Holy Spirit's acting in a person's life and to wait for the right opportunity to speak. Thankfully we are not left alone with this task—the Holy Spirit will be continuously giving us openings to share our faith. Here are three examples.

One Holy Spirit opportunity occurs when someone asks us why we live the way we do. If we lay down our lives for those around us in sacrificial actions of love and unselfish caring, there is a high probability that someone will say something like this: "I have known you for a while. There seems to be something different about you. What is it? How do you understand this difference?" Questions like these are God-given opportunities for us to respond about our life as a follower of Jesus Christ. We should take full advantage of them.

Another opportunity may come when we find ourselves in the midst of what can only be described as "Holy Spirit coincidences." Consider the biblical story of Philip. The Holy Spirit prompted Philip to head toward the main road to Gaza. He meets an Ethiopian official who is traveling home after visiting Jerusalem and happens to be reading about the suffering servant in the Old Testament. The Holy Spirit prompts Philip to go across and join the chariot. Again he obeys. Overhearing the traveler reading from the book of Isaiah, Philip asks him whether he understands what he is reading. The ensuing conversation goes like this:

> "How can I," [the eunuch] said, "unless someone explains it to me?" So he invited Philip to come up and sit with him. . . . The eunuch asked Philip, "Tell me, please, who is the prophet talking about, himself or someone else?" Then Philip began with that very passage of Scripture and told him the good news about Jesus (Acts 8:31, 34-35).

A third type of opportunity may come when someone expresses a longing for God. It is highly unlikely that he or she will say directly, "I am longing for God. Will you tell me how I can find a relationship with God?" They might say something like, "Something is missing in my life" or "I don't know how I am going to make it through this" or "I wonder what life is all about?" I have realized that if we listen carefully, ask some open ended-questions, and express a genuine interest in what lies beneath the person's words, an opportunity will arise for us to share God's good-news story and our own experience of Christ.

But we first learn to pray, watch, and wait. Witnessing usually moves from the nonverbal to the verbal. When we talk too much, our Christianity may collapse into an empty chattering that fails to penetrate people's hearts. It also reveals a lack of genuine caring in our own heart and cheapens the unsearchable riches of the gospel of Jesus Christ. We learn to be silent in others' presence, attending to their words and watching the Holy Spirit at work in their lives. Only then will we speak words that convey with power God's good-news story and make the amazing love of Jesus a reality for them.

Below is a prayer to help you begin watching and waiting and with which you may want to experiment:

> *Dear God, thank you that your Spirit is already at work in every person that I am going to meet today. Your desire is that every person will hear and respond to your good news. Help me to discern the right time to share my own experience of you. Please grow within me the gifts of the Holy Spirit, especially those of discernment and of wisdom, that I may possess your sense of timing in all that I do and say.*

Every day we find ourselves surrounded by people who desperately need Jesus Christ. Many of them will never enter a church building or attend an evangelical rally or read a religious book. Your life and my life may be the only "Christ" they ever meet. Given the overwhelming needs of the human situation and the deep longings in the human heart, our greatest gift can be our witness to God's good-news story. A weighty challenge faces each one of us: "Are we resolved to become participants in the fellowship of the unashamed?" If we respond yes, we await the Holy Spirit's revealing our next exciting step forward.

QUESTIONS FOR SMALL-GROUP CONVERSATION

Icebreaker: Describe one person whom you consider to be an effective witness to Jesus Christ.

1. In what area of your life do you find it hardest to be a witness to Jesus Christ?
2. How do you feel about talking to others about Jesus Christ?

3. What have you come to know about Christ through your experience of him?
4. In what area in present circumstances might the Holy Spirit be calling you to lay down your life?
5. In what area of your life do you need to grow in order to become a more credible witness to Jesus Christ?

EIGHT

THE GIFT GOD GIVES

. . . Leads Us into the Desert

I shouldn't have done it! I was enjoying supper with a friend when he dared me to run the Comrades Marathon. As most South Africans know, the Comrades is a fifty-five-mile race from Durban to Pietermaritzburg, which attracts runners from around the world. My congregation was building a church sanctuary at that time, and it seemed that running the Comrades could be a great way to raise some much-needed funds. Members would sponsor me per kilometer because they knew I did not run regularly and would probably not finish the race. So I agreed to run.

Five months later I lined up at the start with almost ten thousand other runners. About a month earlier I had qualified by barely finishing a standard marathon in the required time. My preparation had been hopelessly inadequate. I simply had not trained enough. Not surprisingly, when I reached the halfway mark I heard that the winner had already crossed the finish line. I must have looked like I was in trouble, because I remember overhearing an elderly woman say to her friend as I ran past them, "He's not going to make it."

But I did finish. I limped across the finish line just thirty-four seconds before the shot went off indicating the eleven hour cut-off time. I could hardly walk afterward. I still remember hobbling up the steps to board the aircraft to fly home the next day. It took years before I fully recovered from the effects of running such a grueling race in my undertrained condition. Few other experiences have drummed home for me the lesson of living life well: "If we want to be competent on-the-spot we need to do the necessary off-the-spot preparation."[1]

We see this dynamic at work in Jesus' life. Immediately after the Holy Spirit had come upon him at his baptism, the Spirit led him into the wilderness. Only later did the curtain open on his messianic ministry. Gospel writer Luke underlines this important sequence in the way he describes Jesus' Spirit-led journey: "Jesus, full of the Holy Spirit, left the Jordan and was led by the Spirit into the wilderness" (4:1). After this wilderness experience the Gospel tells us that "Jesus returned to Galilee in the power of the Spirit, and news about him spread through the whole countryside" (4:14).

I want to suggest that the Holy Spirit works similarly in our lives. Once we have experienced the Holy Spirit in our conversion, the self-same Spirit will draw us into our own wilderness, or desert, experience. Followers of Jesus throughout the centuries have had these experiences. Like Jesus, if we are going to know the Holy Spirit's power on-the-spot, we require instruction in the wilderness lessons that the Holy Spirit teaches us off-the-spot. The wilderness of the desert becomes the training ground of the Holy Spirit for those who want to live faithfully for the rest of their lives.

Before we explore the work of the Holy Spirit in our own desert experience, I need to explain my use of the word *desert*. Few of us will spend forty days in a tough geographical desert like Jesus did.

However "desert" can serve as a vivid metaphor for those times of solitude when, like Jesus, we are led by the Holy Spirit into a deeper encounter with God and ourselves. In other words, the wilderness of the desert will probably not be for us a literal Sahara-like location that we can find on a map. Most likely, our desert experience will be what Richard Foster calls a "Sahara of the heart"[2] in which the Holy Spirit prepares us off-the-spot for our life of on-the-spot discipleship.

WRESTLING WITH TEMPTATION

I will relate my favorite story about temptation. A man promised God that he would give up eating sweets for Lent. Driving to work one day he saw some delicious-looking cakes in the display window of the local bakery. Immediately he felt the urge to stop and buy one. But he also knew he had committed not to eat sweets or cakes until Easter. In the midst of his internal tug-of-war he decided to put God to the test. "Dear God," he prayed, "if you want me to have this cake let there be a parking space right outside the shop." On his tenth trip around the block, a parking place became available!

Jesus' desert experience was, first and foremost, a time of wrestling with temptation. Three of the Gospel writers tell us that the Holy Spirit led Jesus into the wilderness of the desert where he was tempted by the evil one. (See Matt. 4:1; Mark 1:12; Luke 4:1.) He faced three temptations: to change stones into bread, to throw himself down from the pinnacle of the Temple, to pay homage to the devil. Jesus did not yield to any of them. He refused to focus on the material at the expense of the spiritual. He would not compromise the way of sacrificial self-giving for the glittering option of becoming a religious superstar. He would not exchange his identity as God's beloved for worldly power. When his off-the-spot desert experience concluded, Jesus stood ready for his on-the-spot work as God's Messiah.

How does Jesus' desert experience relate to us? Let me put it like this: During those forty days Jesus did something off-the-spot that we must also do if we are going to be faithful to our God-given vocation on-the-spot. He followed the Holy Spirit into the solitude of the desert where he named and wrestled with his own particular temptations. It was an eye-opening moment for me when I realized that Jesus actually *listened* to what the Tempter had to say. He heard the devil out. He knew that he would be able to resist the evil one only if he remained aware of his tactics. This hidden preparation ensured that Jesus would pattern his public ministry on God's way rather than that of the evil one.

This is just as true for us. If we want to live on-the-spot with God, we need to prepare ourselves off-the-spot. We must allow the Holy Spirit to lead us into our own desert experiences where we can name and wrestle with our personal temptations. As I have already suggested, we will probably face a Sahara of the heart. Our temptations may be less dramatic than those of Jesus, but they will be equally real. They may include our desire to be in control, our tendency to want things to go our way, our inclination to pretend to be what we are not, our compulsion to overwork, and so on. The list is long. Recognizing the specific nature of our own temptations is a significant part of this hidden preparation for faithful discipleship in the public arena of our lives.

WHY IT'S IMPORTANT TO HEAR THE DEVIL OUT

Why is this confrontation with the evil one so critical? Jesus' time of wrestling with temptation reminds us that we all face temptation. Evil thoughts attack each one of us. We all know those invisible influences that try to undermine our relationship with God. We all sometimes experience dark passions and lustful fantasies. When we refuse to face these temptations head-on, they gain more power over our lives. They can easily ambush us; then we end up taking actions that undermine our commitment to be and live as God's people. And, when someone asks us about our actions, we will probably say something like, "I don't know what got into me." For this reason we need to hear what the devil has to say. It creates our awareness of dependence on God's Spirit as tempted human beings.

Let me tell you how the Holy Spirit recently led me into a personal desert-wrestling with temptation. A few months ago my wife, Debbie, told me that the month of May this past year had been for her one of the darkest months in our marriage. I was not surprised. It had been for me a time of huge overcommitment, extreme weariness, and much inner desperation. Debbie stated that the most painful thing for her came in watching me live in this fatigued and fearful state and feeling powerless to change me. I was living beyond my limits, neglecting those closest to me, and seemingly out of tune with God's will for my life. I recognized this difficult conversation as a Holy Spirit moment and decided that I should pay heed or face the consequences. Clearly God was speaking.

A few weeks later I mentioned this observation to my spiritual director. As a wise Jesuit he reminded me that the false spirit sometimes takes on the appearance of an angel of light. He helped me see again that when we have walked with God for a long time, we are seldom tempted by the evil one into blatant sin. More often, we are tempted into good things that pull us away from our true calling. In my case it was all the tasks that engaged me that dark May. Teaching, leading conferences, and counseling hurt people were good things. However, upon closer inspection, the fruit of doing these good things had been not only unhealthy but destructive as well.

Lately I have been asking the Holy Spirit to lead me into the deeper desert of my own heart and shed light on how the evil one might be tempting me at this stage of my life. I have been exploring questions like: Why am I so prone to overcommitment? What are my fears as I grow older? What is it about me that I struggle so much to live into my deepest longings? What form does pride take in my life? By reflecting on such questions the Holy Spirit makes it apparent that some of my good activities are not ones that God desires for me. Instead, they are subtle temptations from the evil one that distract me from the joyful and free life that God wants me to live.

How do you experience temptation at the moment? Will you allow the Holy Spirit to lead you into your own Sahara of the heart to hear the voice of the tempter? Do not be scared to face what rises up from the wilderness of your life. Know that you are not on your own in these desert moments. The same Jesus who overcame the evil one in his wilderness experience is with us as our champion to help us overcome and win through his Spirit. The writer of Hebrews puts it wonderfully:

> We do not have a high priest who is unable to empathize with our weaknesses, but we have one who has been tempted in every way, just as we are—yet he did not sin. Let us then approach God's throne of grace with confidence, so that we may receive mercy and find grace to help us in our time of need (4:15-16).

LEARNING TO LISTEN TO GOD

What do you believe is God's biggest complaint in the Bible? Let me confess that until a few years ago, I would have gotten the answer to this question wrong. When I found the answer, it took me by surprise. You may also be surprised. The answer is not our rebellion. Nor is it our disunity as the people of God. It is not our inability to love fully. It is not our idolatry. While all these matters break God's heart, they are not what God complains about the most in scripture. The correct answer? *We do not listen to God.* The words *listen* and *hear* appear more than fifteen hundred times in the Bible. One scholar by the name of Klyne Snodgrass studied each of these passages and came to the realization that the freely chosen deafness of God's people is the biggest complaint recorded in scripture.[3]

When Jesus was asked about the greatest commandment, he quoted the Shema from the Old Testament. "Hear, O Israel . . . Love the Lord your God" (Deut. 6:4-5). Notice that the word *hear* comes *before* the command to love. The prior command is the command to listen, the first duty of love. We can only love God (and this applies to loving others too) when we learn the art of listening. Everything falls into its proper place in our relationship with God when we learn to listen to God and then practice what God says to us.

Jesus pursued this course in his desert experience. He listened to God speaking to him. He then responded to each temptation with words God had spoken to God's people in the past. When he was tempted to turn stones into bread, he answered that human beings cannot live on bread alone. When he was tempted to give his allegiance to the evil one, he answered that we must worship God alone. When he was tempted to jump from the highest point of the Temple and let the angels catch him, he answered that we must not put the Lord our God to the test. In a nutshell: Jesus listened to what Abba told him off-the-spot, which shaped everything he did on-the-spot.

GOD'S WORD AND GOD'S SPIRIT

We can learn from Jesus' example in the wilderness. There he shows us that God's Word and God's Spirit combine together off-the-spot to prepare us for victorious living on-the-spot. Some time ago I came across three sentences that underline this divine partnership in the maturing and deepening of our lives with God.

When we focus only on God's Word, we dry up. When we focus only on God's Spirit, we blow up. But when we focus both on God's Word and God's Spirit, we grow up.[4]

This was true for Jesus; it is true for us. Like Jesus, we need to follow the Holy Spirit's leading into our own desert where we can
listen to what God has to say to us. Only then will we live faithfully
with God in the midst of our everyday trials and temptations.

Where and how does God speak? God mainly speaks to us
through the scriptures. God spoke to Jesus in the desert using this
method. But, you may say, the tempter also used words from the
Bible when he attacked Jesus in the desert. You are correct. Tempting us to use the words of the Bible wrongly is one of the devil's
favorite tactics. Too many of us use the words of scripture to support
attitudes and actions that actually break God's heart. We can read
the Bible and accumulate lots of Bible information and completely
miss the life-giving word that comes from God. This is what Jesus
meant when he said to the religious professionals of his day: "You
study the Scriptures diligently because you think that in them you
have eternal life. These are the very Scriptures that testify about me,
yet you refuse to come to me to have life" (John 5:39-40).

We depend on the Holy Spirit when we read the Bible. The
Holy Spirit changes our relationship with the Bible from mere reading for the sake of getting more information into a living encounter
with the speaking God. We distinguish between God and the Bible,
between the Person and the paper, between the Word and the words.
They are not the same. Failure to see the difference can result in
tragedy. As one writer has pointed out, it is like reading the story of
Jonah, trying to figure out if a human being could live inside a whale,
and what kind of whale it was—yet never actually encountering the
God of Jonah and the whale.[5] But when we read the Bible with the
help of God's Spirit, we open ourselves to the God who personally
communicates with us and meets us in and through the Bible.

Let us consider what this may mean in practice. When we try
to read the Bible in order to listen to God, we need to ask the Holy
Spirit to help us hear what God is saying. We remind ourselves that
the Holy Spirit, who inspired the original author to write what we

are about to read, is the self-same Holy Spirit who works in us as we read. After we have asked for the Holy Spirit's help, we then read the selected passage slowly, thoughtfully, meditatively. We wait for a word or a phrase or a sentence to catch our attention. Then like a cow chewing the cud, we turn the words over and over again, drawing them deep into our hearts and minds. When this process begins, we find that the Holy Spirit is at work, bringing God's personal word into our lives that very moment.

This kind of Bible reading must be bathed in a time of prayerful wondering, thoughtful reflection, and creative brooding. We wonder aloud with God about what the Holy Spirit may be saying to us. We think carefully about what God's word might mean for our daily lives. As products of our time and society, we need an awareness of the ease with which we distort the meaning of scripture to suit the dominant assumptions of our culture. So we brood, like a hen sitting on eggs, over what has stood out for us, asking the Holy Spirit to help us carefully disentangle God's message from our own prejudices and cultural baggage. When we finish our meditation on scripture and go about our daily tasks, we take this personal word from God with us. We let it percolate within us throughout the day. The Holy Spirit uses God's alive and powerful word to form and transform our thinking and living.

The desert moments of listening to God provide an important ingredient in our off-the-spot preparation for our life with God on-the-spot. The Old Testament book of Hosea encourages this preparation: "I am now going to allure her; I will lead her into the desert and speak tenderly to her" (Hos. 2:14). This image describes God's intimate wooing back of the faithless marriage partner so God may speak to her. So too the Holy Spirit woos us into the quietness of our own hearts, where God can speak to us. I hope we will follow these promptings of the Holy Spirit. Because the lessons of the desert are never finished, we should expect the Holy Spirit to take us there again and again.

BEING MINISTERED TO BY ANGELS

I recently led a Quiet Day for about twenty people at a nearby retreat house. They came from different cultural, age, and work backgrounds: business people, homemakers and mothers, retired men and women, and students. They ranged in age from about twenty to sixty-five. As I often do at the beginning of such an event, I asked each person to introduce himself or herself by telling the group what had brought him or her to the retreat. As we went around the circle I was struck by how many times I heard words like *tired, exhausted, burnt out, weary*. Obviously, three-quarters of those present had come in need of refreshment and renewal.

We identify with this desire. We live full and hectic lives. From early in the morning, we stay busy with deadlines to meet, tasks to complete, children to care for, shopping to do, meetings to attend, people to see, e-mails to answer, people to entertain. The wearying list goes on and on. The mental and physical effects of this frantic overactivity range from tiredness to weariness to burnout. But there are also dangerous spiritual consequences. We can find ourselves depleted of inner resources, running on empty and out of touch with God. As a result, we are often more liable to give in to the temptations that seek to trip us up each day. Weariness makes us vulnerable to the evil one!

Jesus' wilderness time speaks into our tired, weary, and exhausted lives. While his desert experience was a time of inner wrestling and testing, it was much more than that. It was also a space in which he was refreshed, renewed, and reenergized by the Holy Spirit for his calling as God's Messiah. Sometimes we think that Jesus was at his weakest when God allowed him to be tempted by the evil one, but this does not seem to be true. Two of the Gospel writers tell us that angels ministered to him. (See Matt. 4:11; Mark 1:13.) Strengthened off-the-spot by the Holy Spirit and the angels, Jesus moved forward to deliver others from the power of evil on-the-spot.

Significantly, when we put Jesus' temptation story within the bigger story of God's people, the strengthening role of the desert in our lives becomes even clearer. For example, in the Old Testament, Israel found its identity reaffirmed in the empty space of the wilderness (Deut. 32:10). There too Israel's renewal took place; the desert rejoiced and blossomed like the crocus, and waters flowed again. (See Isa. 35:1-6.) The biblical image of the desert's experience of testing and trial makes a strong connection with that of refreshment and renewal. Certainly for Jesus the wilderness time offered temptation *and* strengthening.

RECEIVING STRENGTH FOR OURSELVES

It can be that way for us too! During the wilderness time those trapped in the barrenness of compulsive busyness receive the ministry of the Holy Spirit and the angels. Those who are tired and weary find rest; those who feel overwhelmed discover fresh vitality; those caught up in empty lives receive words from the Lord by which to live; those who have lost all sense of identity receive the assurance that they are God's beloved. The Holy Spirit will lead us into our own desert experience so that we can be strengthened. This becomes our off-the-spot preparation for God-faithfulness on-the-spot.

One person who found herself strengthened in her own wilderness time is Dr. Mamphela Ramphele. In her reflections on the apartheid years of South Africa, she describes how her immersion in the liberation struggle of South Africa brought her to a place of emotional and physical exhaustion. In 1990 she began to experience inner tension as she tried to balance the competing demands of single parenthood with social activism. In the midst of her burnout her spiritual director, Father Ted King, persuaded her to spend a few days in solitude and silence. She spent this time walking, sleeping, reading, and reflecting. She ended her time apart by sharing in the parish Eucharist at the Kalk Bay Anglican Church. Her reflections underscore how the angels minister to us to restore our energy and vitality when we allow the Holy Spirit to lead us into our own desert experience. She notes the importance of this time: "I could restore myself to myself."[6]

In this chapter we have seen that the desert can be a place where the Holy Spirit leads us into a deeper encounter with ourselves and with God. This Sahara of the heart experience can involve us in wrestling with our temptations, listening to God, and being ministered to by the angels. These personal behind-the-scenes activities empower us to remain faithful to Jesus Christ. Being competent on-the-spot requires preparation off-the-spot. This is as true for faithful discipleship as it is for marathon running. So the challenge comes in our response to the leadings of the Holy Spirit to become desert apprentices where we live. If we do, here is a helpful practice.

SOLITUDE AND SILENCE

The practicing of solitude and silence obviously helps us cooperate with the desert leadings of the Holy Spirit. We can plan, as regularly as possible, what I like to call a "desert day." We plan to spend as much of a day as possible alone, speaking only to God. Our desert day requires careful consideration for our loved ones, wise arrangements for their welfare, and thoughtful consideration of responsibilities. These matters are important. Those close to us can sometimes feel confused or angry by our decision to spend time in this way. With our awareness of this issue, along with wisdom and sensitivity, we can convey to them why we want to draw apart. Once we have done this, the following practical steps may prove helpful.

The *first step* is to find a suitable place to have a "desert day." The location could be a nearby retreat center, the grounds or facilities of a local church, the quiet backyard of a friend's home, or even your own bedroom if no one is home. You need to decide whether you want this to be a retreat alone or whether you would like to be with a friend. You can experience the silence of solitude on your own or with others. In fact, if you choose a retreat house, other people seeking God in the quiet will likely be there.

The *second step* involves choosing a part of God's good-news story from the Bible in which you can immerse yourself through the day. It could be a story from the Old Testament, a favorite or an unknown psalm, one of Jesus' encounters, a parable, a portion of a letter from the New Testament, or even a theme running through the Bible like all the "I will be with you" sayings. The aim is not to read as much as you can but to listen to what God may be saying to you. It will benefit you to have a notebook or journal in which to record insights that come to you from your engagement with the scriptures, as well as the thoughts that pop into your mind during the silence of the day. Often these thoughts shed light on how the evil one may be tempting you at the moment.

The *third step* comes in structuring the day. Shape the day in such a way that it gives space for you to rest and to relax, to meditate on scripture and to pray, to reflect and to write, to sleep and to eat. Keep your time flexible; the day may change shape as the Holy Spirit leads. Flexibility is always wise when planning a time of solitude and silence, for the Wind blows where it wills.

The *fourth step* is to clarify a general intention for your "desert day." This intention focuses on the strong yearning that you bring to this time apart. The general intention could range from wanting to know God's love more intimately to desiring to intensify your friendship with Jesus to the practical matter of reviewing your priorities and how you spend your time. However you express this intention, always leave room for the surprises of the Holy Spirit. We are not in charge of this time. The Holy Spirit is our true Spiritual Director.

Finally, cultivate a spirit of self-surrender and generous openness. You might allow the words of Mary's prayer, spoken to the angel in the midst of much inner conflict and turmoil, to become your prayer for the day: "I am the Lord's servant. . . . May your word to me be fulfilled" (Luke 1:38). Such a prayer opens our hearts to whatever the Holy Spirit wants to do. Indeed, praying this prayer throughout your "desert day" expresses the kind of trust that makes it possible for the angels to minister to you, just as they did to Jesus.

In the midst of our daily living and loving, our playing and our working, our joys and our struggles, we need to follow the Holy Spirit into our own desert. In that place of testing we can face and be freed from our many falsehoods and facades, and we can begin to find our true security in God. In that place of stillness and inner quiet, we listen to God speaking those words by which we can truly live. The desert becomes a place of renewal and refreshment where the angels come to strengthen us for whatever tasks and trials lie ahead. Little wonder that it is into such a place that the Holy Spirit has drawn people throughout the ages. Will you respond by planning a "desert day" of your own?

SMALL-GROUP CONVERSATION STARTERS

Icebreaker: Describe one experience where you struggled as a result of inadequate preparation off-the-spot.

1. How do you spend time alone with God?
2. In what area of life do you find yourself tempted?
3. How do you listen to God?
4. Where do you find renewal and refreshment?
5. How do you currently experience the Holy Spirit's leading you into the desert?

NINE

THE GIFT GOD GIVES

. . . Engages Us with Suffering

Following Jesus today is challenging. We live in the midst of overwhelming need. The human cries of those who suffer confront us daily: cries of the desperate poor in need of food, shelter, and work; cries of the forgotten elderly in need of thoughtful care; cries of those infected and affected by HIV/AIDS in need of affordable and accessible medication; cries of vulnerable, at-risk children in need of protection and nurture; cries of the violated whose lives have been ripped apart by crime . . . the list goes on. We cannot measure the depth of human need in our society.

I came across a newspaper article recently that put faces to this widespread suffering.[1] It described how four young children from the Mmupele family, ages two, six, seven, and nine, left home to begin an eleven-mile walk in sweltering heat in search of their mother and food. They never reached their destination. When their lifeless bodies were found in the veld, days after they had taken their last walk from the settlement of Verdwaal in North West Province, it was plain to see they had died of hunger and dehydration on a scorching hot day. The story behind their walk was harrowing to read.

The four children had not had a decent meal in weeks. The last of the food in the house, mealie meal borrowed from a neighbor, had run out the previous night. It had only been enough for a bowl of porridge each. The next morning, a pregnant and anxious Kedibone Mmupele, the mother of the children, had awakened early to walk the eleven miles to a nearby farm, where her mother Martha was visiting. She hoped to return with some mealie meal and chicken pieces to feed the children. She told the reporter:

> We were all very hungry because there hadn't been much food in the house for weeks, so by seven that morning I was already on my way to the farm, knowing that I would be home by nightfall.

Soon after Kedibone left home, the children decided to follow her. However, they took a different path and got lost. When she returned home to find her children gone, she was distraught. She said, "I ran around like a mad person, looking for them and shouting their names."

The following day, members of the Community Policing Forum, friends and family searched the neighborhood. Three days later, the two younger children were found dead, sprawled on the ground. They had collapsed from hunger and dehydration and from walking in the heat for so long. With financial assistance from the municipality, the police, and farmers, the children were buried. Meanwhile, the search for the other two children continued. However, the other two children could not be found. A week later a farmer plowing his fields came across their remains. Their bodies, badly decomposed, lay on the ground facing each other.

Kedibone's grief was heightened by the fact that she had no photographs of her children. She expressed her fear that the images of her children's faces would fade from her memory. Nor did any of the children have a birth certificate. The only evidence of their ever having existed were the death certificates issued after they were found. It is hard to imagine this family's suffering.

Does the Holy Spirit care about this kind of human need? Sometimes when we read books about the Holy Spirit, it does not seem so. But our answer must be a resounding yes. In the fourth chapter of Luke we read that when Jesus began his ministry in Nazareth, the Holy Spirit anointed him to proclaim the gospel to the poor, freedom to the oppressed, recovery of sight for the blind, and to set the oppressed free (Luke 4:18-19). Now if the Holy Spirit sent Jesus for this purpose, we can be sure that the same Spirit will draw us into similar tasks in our communities. For this reason I want to emphasize strongly: *The Holy Spirit engages us with suffering.* Let us explore how this might happen for you and me today.

PEOPLE ARE SACRED

I remember the first time I realized the meaning of the familiar closing of worship we call the benediction. It focuses on the most important characteristics of each person of the Trinity. So it speaks of the *grace* of our Lord Jesus Christ, the *love* of God, and then, not the *power* of the Holy Spirit or the *guidance* of the Holy Spirit, or the *light* of the Holy Spirit but the *fellowship* and *communion* of the Holy Spirit. Whatever power and wisdom the Spirit may impart flows from our being made more aware of those around us by the Spirit. This is what the Holy Spirit always seeks to do in our lives: generate awareness of people's sacredness and so lead us into a deeper shared life with others in their needs and in their suffering.[2]

This sacred awareness of people is a trait that we are in danger of losing. Way back in the early nineties I remember coleading a workshop with the late Aggrey Klaaste who served then as editor of *The Sowetan*. We were reflecting together with a group of people drawn from around Southern Africa on the challenges of spirituality, doing justice, and nation-building. Referring to a recent editorial in which he had commented on the desecration of graves, Aggrey made a comment that I believe was prophetic:

> *We have lost a sense of the sacredness of human life. If we are going to build a new nation, we will need to rediscover that each person we meet is a sacred human being.*

God's good-news story challenges us in this same way. Throughout the Gospels the actions and sayings of the Spirit-filled Jesus of Nazareth are characterized by his profound awareness of the sacredness of people. Whether he conveyed this sacredness by hugging a child nagging for attention, sitting down for a meal with a politically incorrect tax collector, touching an outcast leper, showing unconditional acceptance to a used and abused prostitute, or receiving help from a person of another race, Jesus treated each individual with immense respect and care.[3] People sensed that they mattered to Jesus; each person he met came to realize his or her infinite worth to God.

Jesus' words supported his actions. Listen in on his conversation with his disciples as he compares people to the birds of the air: "Are not two sparrows sold for a penny? Yet not one of them will fall to the ground outside your Father's care. And even the very hairs of your head are all numbered. So don't be afraid; you are worth more than many sparrows" (Matt. 10:29). Imagine the life-affirming effect these words would have had on the lives of the early Christ-followers. Without doubt they would have known that they mattered to Jesus and the God he embodied.

BECOMING AWARE

When the Spirit of Christ touches our lives, we too become more aware of the sacredness of every human being. As the Spirit filled Jesus and made him the most responsive human being who ever lived, so his Spirit generates in us a similar current of awareness. We begin to see the image of God in our neighbor. We become more conscious of each person's value to God. We gradually move out of our isolated world through a new interest in and concern for others. This comes through the Holy Spirit's work in us, which makes us more aware of those around us, revealing their sacredness to us. In this way the Spirit draws us into a genuine communion with others in their pain. In our suffering world, few things are more revolutionary and healing than this.

How open are you to this awareness-generating work of the Spirit? We need to confess that ingrained habits of heart and mind block the Holy Spirit. In my own experience I can think of qualities like my selfishness and self-centeredness, my deep-rooted apathy to other people's needs, my cynicism about people's motives, my fear about moving into the world of other people, my tendency to measure others by appearance and economic status. This list is not exhaustive. Think about your life at the moment. What hinders the Holy Spirit from revealing to you the sacredness of those around you? You may want to speak about this with God.

It is not easy to live daily with this divine revelation of the sacredness of every human being. We simply cannot bear the weight of the infinite preciousness of each individual on our own. But we can trust the Holy Spirit to initiate this kind of awareness within us. We need God's love to flow into our lives and through them. This is the work of God's Spirit who, as Paul reminds us, pours

God's love into our lives. (See Rom. 5:5.) Perhaps right now, you may want to ask the Holy Spirit to baptize you into this love of God in a more profound way. You can be sure that this will sharpen your awareness of the sacredness of your nearest neighbors like nothing else. You can also rest assured that you will soon find yourself engaged with their suffering. This is the Holy Spirit at work in your life!

BEING WITH

I remember with some embarrassment my first attempts to lessen the suffering of people in my hometown. I had been following Jesus for a few months, reading the New Testament letter of James, and beginning to learn about the relationship between faith and works. Some sentences that really haunted me in those days, and continue to do so today, were those halfway through the second chapter, where James writes about the uselessness of going to those who have no clothes or daily food and wishing them well with empty words. Such faith without deeds is dead. These words called me into action.

Philip, my friend who first introduced me to the Jesus-story, and I would go to parties on Friday nights, armed with brown paper bags. While everyone was dancing in the darkness, we would fill our bags with chips and sandwiches from the food tables. Then we would slip out and make our way to the inner-city streets of Port Elizabeth where the homeless slept in the doorways of the closed shops. Without bothering to get to know anyone's name or listen to anyone's story, we would give away our stolen goods as quickly as we could. Once we completed this task, we would head home, hoping that we had done what God required! The next Friday night we would repeat the process.

I do not want to come down too hard on these early attempts to follow Jesus. Yes, I was guilty of taking food that was not mine.

Yes, I realize now that I was condescending, insensitive, and thought-less in those encounters with the homeless. But looking back, I believe the Holy Spirit was stirring up in my heart a desire that would stay with me for the rest of my life: the desire to get involved with those who suffer. I had to learn that for this engagement to have dignity and integrity, the Spirit needed to show me how to *be with* those who suffer. Only then would I begin to experience the communion of the Holy Spirit.

To catch a glimpse of how the Holy Spirit enables us to be with persons who suffer, let me contrast my first attempts to engage suffering with another story. It goes like this: A West Indian woman in a London flat was told of her husband's death in a street accident. The shock of such unexpected grief stunned her. She sank into a corner of the sofa and sat there rigid and unhearing. For a long time her terrible trancelike look embarrassed her family, friends, and officials who came and went. Then the school teacher of one of her children, an English woman, called on the family. The teacher sat down beside the wife and put an arm around her tight shoulders. A white cheek touched a brown one. Then as the unrelenting pain seeped through to her, the newcomer's tears began to flow quietly, falling on their two hands linked in the woman's lap. For a long time that was all that took place. Then at last the West Indian woman began to sob. Still not a word was spoken. After a while the visitor got up and left, leaving her monetary contribution to help the family meet its immediate practical needs. John Taylor, who tells this story, reflects almost poetically:

> *This is the embrace of God, his kiss of life. That is the embrace of his mission, and of our intercession. And the Holy Spirit is the force in the straining muscles of an arm, the film of sweat between pressed cheeks, the mingled wetness on the backs of clasped hands. He is as close and as unobtrusive as that, and as irresistibly strong.*[4]

This powerful incident reminds me of another instance. I was called to the hospital to be with a mother and father whose baby was stillborn. Their grief was raw and anguished. In situations like these I often run out of words. I had little to say or do. I simply remained with them, trusting that through my silent presence, the Holy Spirit would bring comfort into their broken hearts. I do not know if this occurred or not. I do know that some days later I received a card from them with the words, "Thank you for being with us in our time of desperate need."

Will you join me in letting the Holy Spirit show us how to be with those who suffer? It will save us from a toxic charity that sometimes dehumanizes more than it helps. It will make possible a giving of ourselves uncontaminated by empty words and loveless actions. It will set us free from a cold and misdirected activism that seldom dignifies the lives on whose behalf we seek to bring justice. It will make us continual learners who never assume that we are experts in knowing what the other person needs. But perhaps most importantly, it will provide a foundation from which we can engage those who suffer—engage them with Spirit-inspired words and Spirit-directed actions that bring life and blessing.

SPEAKING AND DOING

There comes the time when, in our engagement with suffering, we must go beyond just being present with those in need. In order to bless and to bring life to those who are oppressed and in pain, we allow the Holy Spirit to speak and act through us. When we read through the New Testament, the Spirit does this in two chief ways. Sometimes the Holy Spirit *transforms our human abilities;* at other times the Holy Spirit *transcends our human inabilities.*[5] Both are ways in and through which the Holy Spirit empowers us to be part of God's good-news story today in a broken and hurting world.

We see this especially in the book of Acts after the Holy Spirit had come upon the first Christ-followers at Pentecost. These early disciples, like Jesus himself, did not hold any recognized positions of power. They were not part of any influential religious or political organization. They really were a group of "nobodies." Yet they turned their world upside down for good within two decades because the Holy Spirit transformed their natural abilities and transcended their natural inabilities. Therefore, just like Jesus, who was anointed by the Holy Spirit with power to do good and to heal all who were under the power of evil, so were they.

Take some time to read through the book of Acts if you want to see how the Holy Spirit worked through the early Christ-followers' speaking and doing. When they proclaimed God's good-news story, the Holy Spirit brought many into God's family. When they shared their material possessions, the Holy Spirit blessed people in need. When they ministered to the sick and lame, the Holy Spirit gave remarkable gifts of healing. When they reached out to people from different cultural backgrounds, the Holy Spirit created a new kind of community that had not been seen before in the first-century world. When they opposed unjust practices, the Holy Spirit set people free. When you step into the fifth book of the New Testament, you see how the Spirit transformed these early Christians' human abilities and transcended their human inabilities as they engaged their suffering world.

THREE CONTEMPORARY STORIES

The Holy Spirit continues to do this today. Let me share three stories. First, I think of a good friend of mine who serves as the human resources director in a medium-sized company that employs about six hundred people. He knows most employees by name. He visits their homes when tragedy strikes and advocates on behalf of the workers for a more equitable sharing of profits. He creates jobs wherever he can. He has set up training programs to empower and to equip those who were previously disadvantaged. Recently he facilitated a wage agreement for the next three years, which was agreed upon by the workers involved. I am amazed at how the Holy Spirit transformed his natural abilities for the sake of the common good. Yet he also tells me that the outcomes of his efforts have far exceeded what he could have achieved in his own strength and wisdom. Without a doubt, the Holy Spirit has been at work!

The second story comes from the classroom of my wife. Early this year Debbie asked learners in one of her new classes about their dreams for the future. Lerato shared her wish that all the teachers in the school be killed. Debbie, while taken aback, offered a Spirit-inspired response. She decided to greet Lerato each morning by name. She went out of her way to express interest in her life. She affirmed her as often as she could. One day Lerato asked Debbie if they could speak privately. During break time Lerato told about her painful past of abuse, neglect, and struggle with poverty. From that conversation onward Lerato's attitude changed totally. Today Lerato is one of the best learners in the class. I view this shift as the Holy Spirit at work, transforming Debbie's teaching abilities and changing another person on the inside.

The third story involves a pastoral encounter I had with someone who felt completely forsaken by God. Early one Friday morning, a friend brought a suicidal woman to my office. For over two hours I listened to her dark and desperate story. I felt totally inadequate to know how to respond. Before she left, I asked if we could pray together. As we sat together silently before praying, three letters came into my mind. They were BOB. I asked her if this meant anything. She recounted a horrific story of rape by someone named Bob. I told her that I believed the Holy Spirit had given this name to me as a reminder that God understood and had not forgotten what had happened to her. This moment became a turning point in her relationship with God and in her struggle with despair. The Holy Spirit had transcended my human inability to help someone in a life-and-death situation by giving me a piece of information to share with her that I could not possibly have known by myself.

As the Holy Spirit helps us engage those who suffer, we can depend on the same Spirit to bring life and blessing through us. Whatever our speaking and doing abilities may be, the Holy Spirit can transform them. They could be our computer competency, our leadership strength, our organizational capacity, our people skills, our homemaking talent, or many other aptitudes. The Holy Spirit can set them on fire! But let us also remind ourselves that the Holy Spirit can transcend our human inabilities with *special* abilities that come from God. The Spirit can give us special grace-gifts[6] of knowledge and wisdom, of healing and miraculous powers, of discernment and prophecy for particular situations. We would be wise to learn as much as we can about how these grace-gifts operate and to convey an openness to them.

PLANNED ENCOUNTERS WITH PEOPLE WHO SUFFER

Throughout this book I have stressed that it is the Holy Spirit who changes us inwardly. The Holy Spirit replaces our hearts of stone with hearts of flesh and makes us aware of the sacredness of neighbor. The Holy Spirit pours the love of God into our lives. Inner transformation is always the gift and work of God's Spirit. Yet I have also tried to make it clear that we are not passive passengers on this journey. We can employ certain practices that open our lives more fully to this transforming work. I want to close this chapter by describing one such practice that few books on spiritual disciplines mention: *planned encounters with people who suffer*.

We need to keep both sides of this practice in mind. On the one hand, because we can easily avoid the suffering of people around us, we need proactive planning to be with them. For this reason I often encourage those young in the faith to make this practice an intentional and regular part of their new life in Christ. Otherwise, it may not happen at all. On the other hand, because we often know about poverty, joblessness, and addiction only in theory, we need flesh-and-blood encounters that confront us with these realities. Tragically, we seldom share deeply with or learn from those who understand these painful circumstances firsthand. But when we do share, we often meet people who resiliently refuse to give in to hopelessness. We have much to learn from them.

I encourage you to begin at a simple level. Commit yourself to spend a portion of your week, perhaps an hour, an afternoon, or an evening with someone who suffers. This person may be in prison, terminally ill, severely handicapped, economically poor, or stuck in a dark depression. In my own experience, I have found that the person's name will usually come to you as a result of praying and watching those around you. As you plan to spend time together, keep the following thoughts in mind.

Before getting together, ask the Holy Spirit to be with you in the encounter. When you are with the person, make sure that the emphasis of your time together stresses your being with the other person. Be present as simply as you can. Be aware of that person's sacredness and infinite preciousness to God. Remember that you are there not to give advice or to solve problems—or even to help. You join the person in order to understand what it feels like to be in his or her situation. Your attentive presence is the greatest gift.

During your encounter, try to listen rather than speak. The gift of ears is as important as the gift of tongues. Listening lies at the heart of all our encounters with people in pain. Remind yourself that Christ wants to meet you in the life of this sufferer. He may want to speak to you through this person. So notice your thoughts and feelings as you spend time together, and be alert for the still small voice of God. After the encounter, take time to reflect on your inner responses, perhaps noting them in a journal. Sometimes it can also be helpful for us to talk about these reflections with a soul-friend who listens well. Above all, ask God what you can learn from the experience.

As with any spiritual practice, it will not always be easy to stick with this commitment. You may find yourself looking for excuses to opt out or to put your time to more productive use. If this inner resistance comes along, speak about it with God and maybe with your soul-friend too. I have found that our resistance often reveals to us the hardness of our hearts. These encounters can sometimes bring us face-to-face with the deep-rooted forces of self-centeredness that lurk inside us all. We are not always the compassionate people we think we are. And yet, our acknowledgment before God of this unpleasant reality allows the Holy Spirit to go about quietly trans-forming our hearts.

This spiritual practice is where our Spirit-led journey into an engagement with suffering begins. But it does not end here. As we stick with this practice, divine compassion begins to flower. Non-sentimental and caring deeds are birthed. Courage to speak truth to the "principalities and powers" flowers. Our hearts begin yearning for a society that encourages justice and compassion for all.' This is the Holy Spirit at work, changing us on the inside, engaging us with God's good-news story for our time.

As we endeavor to become more open to the Holy Spirit, we must avoid being drawn into a "spiritual bubble" away from those who suffer. Any form of discipleship that separates us from human need is counterfeit. It betrays God's passionate love for every human being, denies our shared life with one another, and results in what has been described as a "false inwardness." We do not become the person God wants us to be within a private religious zone but within God's broken and wounded world. A life genuinely alive to God's presence will increase our awareness of our neighbor's sacredness, connect us with their tears, and make us responsive to their pain.

Any true work of the Holy Spirit in our lives will engage us more deeply with those who suffer.

SMALL-GROUP CONVERSATION STARTERS

Icebreaker: Describe a time when someone reached out when you found yourself in a difficult situation.

1. What human cry in your surrounding community disturbs you the most right now?
2. What blocks the Holy Spirit from making you more aware of others' sacredness?
3. What does it mean to "be with" someone in his or her pain?
4. Describe one experience when you realized the Holy Spirit had transformed your human abilities and transcended your human inabilities.
5. Share your specific plans to engage someone in his or her suffering this coming week.

TEN

Experience More of the Gift God Gives

Did the skirt fit? Almost every time I share the story with which I began this book, people come up to me afterward and ask me this question. They may forget the point of my illustration about giving and receiving gifts, but they want to know whether my efforts at cross-dressing in a Zurich boutique were worthwhile or not. So in case you may still be wondering, the answer is yes! When I got home, I gave my gift to Debbie; it fit perfectly, and she has worn it many times.

In this book I have explored two basic questions about the gift that God gives: Who is the Holy Spirit, and what does the Holy Spirit do? In response to the first, I have said that the Holy Spirit is God, lovingly present now and always active in our lives. In response to the second, I have suggested that the Holy Spirit brings us alive to God, draws us into a deeper shared life, changes us inwardly, guides us in our decision making, helps us to pray, empowers us to witness, leads us into the desert, and engages us with suffering. While this list is not exhaustive, I trust you can now better recognize and respond to the Holy Spirit at work in your life.

In this final chapter, I want to explore how we can experience more of this gift. Although the Holy Spirit works in our lives from our very beginnings and especially in our conversion, there is always more of the Holy Spirit to experience. We need no convincing of that. We simply have to look at the massive difference between the transformed lives of those Spirit-filled Christ-followers in the pages of the New Testament and the way we live. The stark contrast between them and us, in loving character and creative power, highlights our need for a fuller experience of the Holy Spirit. Too often in our life with God, we settle for far less than what God has made possible for us in Jesus Christ.

But there is another reason for us to seek more of the Holy Spirit. The New Testament writers encourage us to do so. The writer of Ephesians commanded a group of baptized and active Christ-followers in Ephesus to be filled "with the Spirit" (5:18). He does not deny the Spirit's current activity in their lives but encourages them into a greater participation. If they needed to continue being filled with the Holy Spirit, then so do we!

When I speak of experiencing more of the Holy Spirit, I am not promoting a consumer faith. Genuine life in the Spirit is profoundly other-centered. The Holy Spirit constantly moves us out of our little world of "me, mine, and I" into the large spacious world of God's good-news story. When we begin to seek more of God's gift, we know where the Holy Spirit will lead us. We will be led into a greater responsiveness to Jesus Christ, a sharper awareness of those around us, and a fresh engagement with those who suffer. These consequences are foreign to a privatized spirituality that seeks personal benefits.

How do we go about experiencing more of the Holy Spirit? Our answer does not resemble a divine contract. A contractual approach maintains that God will give us more of the Holy Spirit *only if* we meet certain conditions. It maintains that the Holy Spirit's presence and power are given to us when we have repented enough, prayed enough, claimed enough, fasted enough, waited enough, and so on. But as one of my teachers in these matters has pointed out, such an approach inevitably leads us into an unhealthy preoccupation with ourselves and what we have to do, rather than with God and God's gracious willingness to give us the Spirit. It also threatens the wonderful good news that the Holy Spirit is the gift that God gives us.[1]

Rather than adopting a contractual approach to the question, I want to explore a more relational approach. How do we respond when someone who loves us offers us a gift? We open our hands and receive. To receive the gift that God offers, we unclench our hands and open them. Closed hands say to God, "I don't need your gift. I can live on my own resources. Stand back, God, and watch me!" Open hands say, "I need your gift. I cannot live on my own resources. God, I look to you for what I need." This trusting faith opens our hands to experience more of the Holy Spirit. Three verbs help us unpack this faith. But before I explore them with you, let me tell you about my own experience in this regard.

MY PERSONAL EXPERIENCE

I remember the first time I consciously sought more of the Holy Spirit. Just over three decades ago, I found myself living on the edges of spiritual bankruptcy. The crisis developed in the winter of 1979, against the dark background of apartheid South Africa, when I was ministering in an inner-city congregation in Johannesburg. I had come to the end of my own resources. While continuing daily in the outward motions of ministry, inside I felt bedraggled in spirit, resentful toward those in need, and far from God. One evening, in the middle of this crisis, I wrote out my resignation. It was a moment of terrible sadness and failure because I knew that I had been called into pastoral ministry.

But God, it seemed, had other ideas. Before I could hand in my letter, I found an invitation in our mailbox from a friend. He invited me to attend a three-day retreat at St. Benedict's in Rosettenville, Johannesburg, to be led by an Anglican minister from the UK by the name of Tom Smail. I decided to accept. I still remember Tom's opening address to the thirty of us gathered together. Quoting words that had come to the Old Testament prophet Ezekiel in his vision of the valley of dry bones, "I will put my Spirit in you and you will live" (Ezek. 37:14), he spoke of how God's Spirit breathes new life into barren lives. His words scorched their way into my heart and became God's life-giving word to me.

On the last night all the retreatants were seated in a circle in the chapel. Tom invited anyone who needed the ministry of the Holy Spirit to indicate his or her need. Usually I am reticent about these matters. I looked around the circle. They were all Anglicans! Thankful that none of my Methodist colleagues were present, I got off my chair, knelt on the floor, and held out my open hands. It was my way of taking God's promise to Ezekiel seriously and asking God to make it come true in my life.

One of the people sitting there that night was an Anglican bishop named Peter Lee. He walked across, laid his hands on my bowed head, and prayed a prayer for God to fill me from the tips of my toes to the top of my head with the Holy Spirit. Nothing dramatic took place. I did not feel anything physical happening. But when I got up, I walked outside and found myself whispering to God over and over again, "Abba Father, Abba Father, Abba Father." Looking back today, I believe that the wind of the Holy Spirit blew gently across my life, assuring me that I was indeed loved by God.

When I returned home, I chose not to speak about my experience for at least a year; I wanted to see for myself what would happen. Within a few weeks some significant changes took place. I led someone into a commitment to Jesus Christ for the first time in my life—an incredible joy for me. I acknowledged the final deliverance from a gambling addiction that had held my life in its grip for many years. God, by the power of the Holy Spirit, was doing something in me that I had not been able to do in my own power. People who knew me well also sensed something different in my preaching and teaching, although they could not put their finger on it.

Perhaps most striking, this infilling of the Holy Spirit whetted in me a new appetite for God. I went on my first silent retreat soon after this and found the first scripture passage given to me for meditation to be intriguing. It contained those words from John's Gospel about being thirsty, coming to Jesus, drinking of his Spirit and having streams of living water flowing out from within us. (See John 7:37-39.) These words mirrored my inward experience at that time. With great gratitude I can say that this longing to know God more deeply has never left. It continues to draw me toward God even in those desert moments of dryness and struggle.

Before long I realized that this encounter with the Holy Spirit was simply another step in my journey with Christ. I still had much more of God's Spirit to experience. Fresh future challenges would require fresh fillings. I had to continue being filled with the Holy Spirit. Despite the significance of my time at St Benedict's, I could not live off it forever. I would need to learn how to keep my hands open every day. Three verbs—*Ask, Receive, Live*—have helped me do this. I hope they will help you live with your hands open to God's Spirit.

ASK EXPECTANTLY

Asking lies at the heart of our relationship with God. This bold statement may surprise you. But, as I often tell my congregation, God seldom gate-crashes our lives. Although God has so much to give us, God is never pushy about it. God always respects the freedom in our relationship. Very little with God happens automatically. If you and I desire to be filled with more of the Holy Spirit, we have to ask. Jesus puts it bluntly: "If you then, though you are evil, know how to give good gifts to your children, how much more will your Father in heaven give the Holy Spirit to those who ask him!" (Luke 11:13).

Jesus makes it clear that God immeasurably exceeds those of us who are parents when it comes to love and generosity. God lovingly desires to give us a deeper experience of the intimate presence, the transforming power, and the gracious gifting of the Holy Spirit— and eagerly wants us to experience them. However, God will never force them onto us. We need to ask Abba Father to send us the Holy Spirit and actually expect Abba Father to answer. Asking expectantly opens our hands to God in trusting faith.

Let's face it though; we often struggle as adults to ask for what we need. I remember sitting with a couple who had been married for over twenty years. After I had listened to them speak about their hurts and unmet needs, I asked whether they ever shared their pain with each other and asked one another for what they needed. "I don't ask anyone for anything!" answered the husband. "I'm too scared to ask," responded the wife. I found it very moving to witness this couple break through these barriers of pride and fear, to risk becoming vulnerable and to make their requests. They opened their hands to each other.

How we relate with one another often reflects how we relate to God. Our inability to share our thoughts and feelings honestly and to ask for what we need mirrors our inability to do this with the Divine. Two approaches can help us find a way through this blockage: We can hold in our minds a picture of God as Someone who wants us to experience more of the Holy Spirit, and we can become more aware of our need of God's grace and help in our lives. When these two things come together, asking God for more of the Holy Spirit becomes almost as natural as breathing.

You can begin asking right now. I don't know your situation. Maybe you are facing a new task or a need that calls for a greater empowering from God. Maybe you find yourself going through the motions of believing, and you long for a fresh sense of life and immediacy in your relationship with God. Maybe you have come to the end of your own resources, and you need to experience strength from beyond yourself. Maybe your bones are dry, and you need God to breathe new life into you. Take some time to think again about those words of Jesus, "How much more will your Father in heaven give the Holy Spirit to those who ask him!" Let this promise give birth to a prayer of request.

> *Abba Father, I thank you for your Spirit's presence in my life. But I need to experience you much more deeply. Breathe your breath on me so that I may bring life to others. Release the power of your Spirit in my inner being, so that Christ may truly live in me. Show me people with whom I can learn how to become open each day to the presence of your Holy Spirit. I ask this in the name of Jesus, through whom you promised me your own Spirit. Amen.*

Will you open your hands and ask expectantly?

RECEIVE THANKFULLY

But receiving the Holy Spirit goes far beyond asking! Asking alone can create passivity in our walk with God. We also have to trust the reality of the promise made to us and receive what we have been offered. Trusting faith opens our hands to take hold of what Abba Father has promised. Remember that encounter between the risen Jesus and his frightened disciples in the upper room? Jesus came into their midst, extended his peace to them, and commissioned them to go into the world as he had been sent. Then he breathed on them and said, "Receive the Holy Spirit" (John 20:22).

Sometimes when addressing a group, I try to underline the importance of receiving with the following illustration. I stop speaking, look at the audience, and say, "Could someone give me a Bible?" Three or four people will usually come forward and offer me their Bible. I ignore their offers and keep on asking for a Bible. Eventually, many people with Bibles in their hands surround me, but I continue to walk around asking for one. Finally I explain, "When we ask for something, we must then be willing to receive it. It's the same in our relationship with God. If we ask for more of the Holy Spirit, we must learn how to receive."

It is a beautiful thing to see relationships in which asking and receiving are a joyful and loving part of being together. This is how good relationships work. Think for a moment. When we are close to someone, we feel free to ask for what we need and a willingness to receive what is given. The simplest way for us to receive what is given to us in love is to open our hands, say thank-you, and make the gift part of our lives. When we give a gift to someone and this does not happen, we wonder whether what we have given has truly been received. Perhaps this is why we teach our children to say both "please" *and* "thank-you."

When we ask Abba Father for more of the Holy Spirit, we receive thankfully. Our thanksgiving does not have to be elaborate. We simply say, "Thank you, Lord, for the gift of your Spirit," and we mean it. We take time to dwell on the thought that the Holy Spirit is living and breathing and praying in our lives. We see our bodies as temples of the Spirit. We affirm that Christ *does* dwell in our hearts through his Spirit. When we receive the Holy Spirit in this thankful way, we begin to live with a deeper consciousness of God's loving and active presence in our lives moment by moment.

Other things may also happen as we receive God's gift, but it is important that we place no rules on this experience. The Spirit of God always works uniquely in our lives. Some people feel a new sense of closeness to Christ; others sense a renewed desire to read scripture or to pray. Others develop a greater responsiveness to suffering; some claim victory over a bad habit or release from an addiction. A number of people display an uncharacteristic boldness in standing for truth and justice; others experience a new freedom in worship and praise. Whatever it may be, the common factor comes in experiencing God the Holy Spirit in some way beyond what we have previously known.[2]

It also helps to remember that not all comings of the Holy Spirit are sudden, dramatic, and sensationally transforming. Sometimes they may be slow, quiet, and spread over time. The Holy Spirit comes in many different ways—not only in intense moments of prayer and worship but in every breath we take, every meal we share, every hug we get, every flower we look at; indeed, in everything that is good and beautiful and true. God's Holy Spirit accompanies every gift that we are given to enjoy. Receive the gift of God, where you are, right now.

Will you open your hands and receive thankfully?

LIVE LOVINGLY

When we ask Abba Father to send us the Holy Spirit, we keep in mind that we do so in the name of Jesus Christ. Matters go badly when people who do not intend to be Jesus' disciples ask God for the Holy Spirit. These persons seek spiritual thrills that contradict God's good-news story. We genuinely ask the Holy Spirit to fill us only when we trust Jesus with our whole lives.

Scripture supports this truth. Jesus always links the giving of the Holy Spirit to loving obedience and being in relationship with him. On one occasion he said, "If you love me, keep my commands. And I will ask the Father, and he will give you another advocate to help you and be with you forever—the Spirit of truth" (John

14:15-17). Certainly Peter understood it this way. In one of his sermons he states that God gives the Holy Spirit to those who obey. (See Acts 5:32.) Following Jesus immerses us in the ethos of the Holy Spirit. Our intention to obey Jesus in every part of our lives is the engine that pulls the train of living in the Spirit.[3]

Now obedience to Jesus Christ is expressed in both his big words and in his little words. I am sure you know the big words. "Love the Lord your God with all your heart and with all your soul and with all your mind. . . . And the second is like it: 'Love your neighbor as yourself'" (Matt. 22:37, 39). Then there are the little words that illustrate the big words at work in specific situations. "Bless those who curse you"; "do not judge"; and "love your enemies."[4] Perhaps you can begin your journey into obedience to Christ with the big words with your nearest neighbor. As you do, you can be sure that Jesus in the power of his Spirit will come alongside you and strengthen you for the task.

PRACTICE MAKES POSSIBLE

But what does all this mean in practice? Throughout this book I have described simple practices designed to bring our lives into direct, personal interaction with Christ through his Spirit. Here is another one you may like to try:

List two or three neighbors with whom you are most intimately engaged. Most probably they will be people in your family. It could be your partner, your child, your parent, your brother or sister. The circle can get bigger as you go along. Be realistic as you do this exercise, and watch out for sentimental abstractions. Then give much thought, attention, and prayer to how you can serve these nearest neighbors in a loving way. Remember, we love our neighbor when we extend ourselves for his or her good. Allow time for this to grow. It may probably take a few months until it becomes a Holy

Spirit-empowered habit. Then you can include more people in the circle of your effective neighbor-love.[5]

If my experience represents this practice fairly, you will feel totally inadequate for the task. The reality is, We *are* inadequate. But this inadequacy is okay. The needs of others are often too great for our own resources. If we try to do things on our own, the result will sometimes be failure, burnout, and perhaps even some kind of breakdown. So what can we do? In our inadequacy we will need to keep our hands open to the love of God that flows into our lives through the Holy Spirit. The only way I know of doing this is to live in the ongoing interplay of the aforementioned three verbs: *Ask-Receive-Live.*

For the past few months I have been meeting with a successful businessman who struggles to love. There are reasons for this, ranging from his own loveless home background to some brutal and terrifying experiences as an eighteen-year-old conscript in the military. For the past few months he has committed himself to one or two specific loving actions in his closest relationships. These usually involve careful thought, much courage, and some risk. We also together ask the Holy Spirit to help him put this commitment into practice. It has been very moving to witness God's Spirit helping him to love in a way that he has never loved before.

Will you open your hands and live lovingly?

A CLOSING VISION

I would like to end by holding before you the vision I have tried to paint in these chapters of your life and mine indwelled by the Holy Spirit. I hope that it will evoke in you deep desire, fresh intention, and thoughtful action. Here is the vision. Think of how it may apply to your life—where you are right now.

When we are filled with the Holy Spirit, we come alive to God, to other people, to ourselves, and to the world in which we live.

We will experience in our hearts and minds a fresh responsiveness to God's good-news story in the scriptures and to the life of prayer; to the living Jesus Christ as our Savior, friend, teacher, and Lord present in our midst; to the sacredness of the person next to us; to the potential and possibilities of living our lives as partners with God; to both the beauty and the brutality of our world; and to the greatness and goodness of God in and through it all.

When we are filled with the Holy Spirit, we will be changed from one level of glory to another. The growing fruit of the Holy Spirit in our characters that is both transformed and being transformed will give evidence of God at work. There will be a fragrance of Christ about our presence. Our deepest attitudes and responses to others will be those of Jesus, because we have learned to let his Spirit grow his life in us. The fruit of Christ's living in us through the Holy Spirit will be visible signs of "love, joy, peace, forbearance, kindness, goodness, faithfulness, gentleness and self-control" (Gal. 5:22-23).

When we are filled with the Holy Spirit, we will have rich results, clearly beyond those of our own efforts. Our human abilities will be transformed and our human inabilities transcended by the power of the Holy Spirit at work in us. Healing and blessing will flow from our being, our words and our doing into the lives of those suffering around us. There will be a powerful strength to our lives in times of trial, temptation, and tragedy. When we are weak, we will be made strong.

When we are filled with the Holy Spirit, we will share in an eternal fellowship of loving people indwelled by a good and beautiful trinitarian God. Heaven will start to become a reality on earth, beginning with our own lives. Indeed, our ultimate destiny, in the mind-stretching words of Dallas Willard, is to be "absorbed in a tremendously creative team effort, with unimaginably splendid leadership, on an inconceivably vast plan of activity, with ever more comprehensive cycles of productivity and enjoyment." This is what the "eye hath not seen, neither the ear heard" that lies ahead of us in the prophetic vision.[6]

This vision for our lives is made possible by God in Jesus Christ through the Holy Spirit. Each one of us has received glimpses and foretastes of it in different ways and in different degrees. We cannot make this vision happen, manufacture it, or master it. We must decide whether to live with open hands or clenched fists. I pray that we will ask expectantly, receive thankfully, and live lovingly as followers of Jesus Christ.

SMALL-GROUP CONVERSATION STARTERS

Icebreaker: What gift have you received from your time in the group over these past few weeks?

1. How would you describe your present experience of the Holy Spirit?
2. Would you describe your experience with the Holy Spirit in contractual or relational terms?
3. How do you feel about asking for what you need?
4. What does it mean for you to receive the Holy Spirit more deeply into your life?
5. Share your present need for the Holy Spirit in your life and take time in your group praying for one another.

NOTES

INTRODUCTION

1. John V. Taylor, *A Matter of Life and Death* (London: SCM, 1986), 15.

ONE: THE GIFT GOD GIVES

1. I develop this idea in the first chapter of *Signposts to Spirituality: Towards a Closer Walk with God* (Cape Town: Struik Christian Books, 2007).

2. Raneiro Cantalamessa first made me aware of the close relationship between the Holy Spirit and grace. He explores this connection in his book, *Come, Creator Spirit: Meditations on the Veni Creator* (Pretoria: Protea Books, 2003). Have a look at some of the New Testament passages where you find the word *grace*. In many cases you could replace the word with *the Holy Spirit* and the meaning of the sentence would remain similar, e.g., Acts 11:23; Romans 12:6; 2 Corinthians 12:9.

3. See passages such as these: 1 Corinthians 12:3; John 3:5; 1 Corinthians 2:10-11.

TWO: BRINGS US ALIVE TO GOD'S PRESENCE

1. In seeking to develop a better understanding of God's good-news story, I have been greatly helped by the writings of Dallas Willard, N. T. Wright, and Scot McKnight.

2. Gerard W. Hughes, *Oh God, Why? A Spiritual Journey Towards Meaning, Wisdom and Strength*, 2nd ed. (Abingdon, Oxfordshire: Bible Reading Fellowship, 2000), 31–35.

THREE: DRAWS US INTO A DEEPER SHARED LIFE

1. The phrase "imposter of the Spirit" comes from the writings of Brennan Manning.

FOUR: TRANSFORMS US INWARDLY

1. I came across this illustration in Donald Nicholl's book, *Holiness* (London: Darton, Longman, and Todd, 1981), 3.

2. The phrase *little Christ* comes from George MacDonald's prayer, "O Christ, my life, possess me utterly. Take me and make a little Christ of me." I found this prayer in *Jesus Manifesto: Restoring the Supremacy and Sovereignty of Jesus Christ*, Leonard Sweet and Frank Viola (Nashville, TN: Thomas Nelson, 2010), 172.

3. I have explored these ideas more fully in *Signposts to Spirituality*, Struik Christian Books, revised edition 2007, 81–83.

4. This story can be found in John Claypool's *Opening Blind Eyes* (Nashville, TN: Abingdon Press, 1983), 61.

5. Mark Gibbard writes about these two categories of prayer in his book, *Love and Life's Journey: Venture in Prayer* (Oxford: Mowbray, 1987).

FIVE: GUIDES US IN OUR DECISION MAKING

1. David Lonsdale, *Eyes to See, Ears to Hear: An Introduction to Ignatian Spirituality* (London: Darton, Longman and Todd, 1995), 65.

2. Samuel Wells, *Improvisation: The Drama of Christian Ethics* (Grand Rapids, MI: Brazos Press, 2004).

3. Marva J. Dawn, Eugene Peterson, *The Unnecessary Pastor: Rediscovering the Call* (Grand Rapids, MI: Wm. B. Eerdmans Publishing Co., 2000), 30.

4. James Martin, *The Jesuit Guide to (Almost) Everything: A Spirituality for Real Life* (New York: HarperCollins, 2010).

5. Lonsdale, *Eyes to See*, 69.

SIX: HELPS US TO PRAY

1. Albert Nolan, *Jesus Today: A Spirituality of Radical Freedom* (Maryknoll, NY: Orbis Books, 2006), 71–72.

2. See the writings of Tom Smail and Andre Louf in this regard.

3. Andre Louf, *Teach Us to Pray* (London: Darton, Longman, and Todd, 1992), 21.

4. To begin, you may like to explore Ephesians 1:1-14 and see what this passage has to say about our identity in Christ.

SEVEN: EMPOWERS US TO BE WITNESSES

1. John V. Taylor, *The Go-Between God* (London: SCM Press, 2004), 200.

EIGHT: LEADS US INTO THE DESERT

1. See Dallas Willard, *The Spirit of the Disciplines: Understanding How God Changes Lives* (New York: HarperCollins, 1988) for a fuller exposition of this critical ingredient in the life of the Christ-follower.

2. Richard J. Foster, *Prayer: Finding the Heart's True Home* (New York: HarperCollins, 1992), 18.

3. Scot McKnight refers to the work of Klyne Snodgrass in his book *The Blue Parakeet: Rethinking How You Read the Bible* (Grand Rapids, MI: Zondervan, 2008), 98.

4. These words come from an audiocassette tape of David Watson's teaching on the work of the Holy Spirit.

5. Scot McKnight, *The Blue Parakeet*, 88.

6. Mamphela Ramphele, *A Life*, David Philip, publisher (Cape Town: 1995), 196.

NINE: ENGAGES US WITH SUFFERING

1. *Saturday Star*, 31 October, 2011.

2. Taylor, *The Go-Between God*, 17.

3. See also my book *Signposts to Spirituality*, 84–86

4. Taylor, *The Go-Between God*, 243.

5. Scot McKnight, *One Life: Jesus Calls, We Follow* (Grand Rapids, MI: Zondervan, 2010), 100.

6. Rather than devote one specific chapter to the grace-gifts of the Holy Spirit, I have woven in stories throughout the book that show them at work in the midst of our daily relational, communal, and missional lives. There are many helpful books written specifically about these grace-gifts. Among the many, I warmly commend Gary Best's *Naturally Supernatural: God May Be Closer Than You Think* (Cape Town, South Africa: Vineyard International Publishing, 2007).

7. Trevor Hudson, *A Mile in My Shoes* (Nashville, TN: Upper Room Books, 2005), 22.

TEN: EXPERIENCE MORE OF THE GIFT GOD GIVES

1. Tom Smail, *The Giving Gift: The Holy Spirit in Person* (London: Hodder and Stoughton, 1988), 17–19.

2. Thomas A. Smail, *Reflected Glory: the Spirit in Christ and Christians* (London: Hodder and Stought some significant changes took place on, 1977), 150.

3. Dallas Willard, *The Great Omission: Reclaiming Jesus's Essential Teachings on Discipleship* (New York: HarperCollins, 2006), 52.

4. We find many of the "small words" in the Sermon on the Mount, Matthew 5–7.

5. This challenge was issued by Dallas Willard at a conference in Benoni, South Africa, in 2010.

6. Dallas Willard, *The Divine Conspiracy: Rediscovering Our Hidden Life in God* (New York: HarperOne, 1998), 399.

More books by

—Trevor Hudson—

and Upper Room Book**s**

The Cycle of Grace: Living in Sacred Balance
(with Jerry P. Haas) #1198

Hope Beyond Your Tears: Experiencing Christ's Healing Love
#1115

The Serenity Prayer: A Simple Prayer to Enrich Your Life
#1094

Questions God Asks Us
#9990

*One Day at a Time: Discovering the Freedom
of 12-Step Spirituality* #9913

A Mile in My Shoes: Cultivating Compassion
#9815

To order go to

bookstore.upperroom.org

or call customer service at

800-972-0433

What Is Renovaré?

Renovaré USA is a nonprofit Christian organization that models, resources, and advocates fullness of life with God experienced, by grace, through the spiritual practices of Jesus and of the historical Church. We imagine a world in which people's lives flourish as they increasingly become like Jesus.

Through personal relationships, conferences and retreats, written and web-based resources, church consultations, and other means, Renovaré USA pursues these core ideas:

- Life with God—The aim of God in history is the creation of an all-inclusive community of loving persons with God himself at the center of this community as its prime Sustainer and most glorious Inhabitant.

- The Availability of God's Kingdom—Salvation is life in the kingdom of God through Jesus Christ. We can experience genuine, substantive life in this kingdom, beginning now and continuing through all eternity.

- The Necessity of Grace—We are utterly dependent upon Jesus Christ, our ever-living Savior, Teacher, Lord, and Friend for genuine spiritual transformation.

- The Means of Grace—Amongst the variety of ways God has given for us to be open to his transforming grace, we recognize the crucial importance of intentional spiritual practices and disciplines (such as prayer, service, confession, or fasting).

- A Balanced Vision of Life in Christ—We seek to embrace the abundant life of Jesus in all its fullness: contemplative, holiness, charismatic, social justices, evangelical, and incarnational.

- A Practical Strategy for Spiritual Formation—Spiritual friendship is an essential part of our growth in Christlikeness. We encourage the creation of Spiritual Formation Groups as a solid foundation for mutual support and nurture.

- The Centrality of Scripture—We immerse ourselves in the Bible: it is the great revelation of God's purposes in history, a sure guide for growth into Christlikeness, and an ever rich resource for spiritual formation.

- The Value of the Christian Tradition—We are engaged in the historical "Great Conversation" on spiritual formation developed from Scripture by the Church's classical spiritual writings.

Christian in commitment, ecumenical in breadth, and international in scope, Renovaré USA helps us in becoming like Jesus. The Renovaré Covenant succinctly communicates our hope for all those who look to him for life:

In utter dependence upon Jesus Christ
as my ever-living Savior, Teacher, Lord, and Friend,
I will seek continual renewal through:
spiritual exercises, spiritual gifts, acts of service.

www.Renovaré.org

8 Inverness Drive East, Suite 102
Englewood, CO 80112 USA
303.792.0152